MIDDLE RHINE
LANDSCAPE PANORAMAS

Photographs by
Barbara and Hartmut Röder

Author
Norbert Marewski

Published by
Helga Neubauer

360° Panoramas

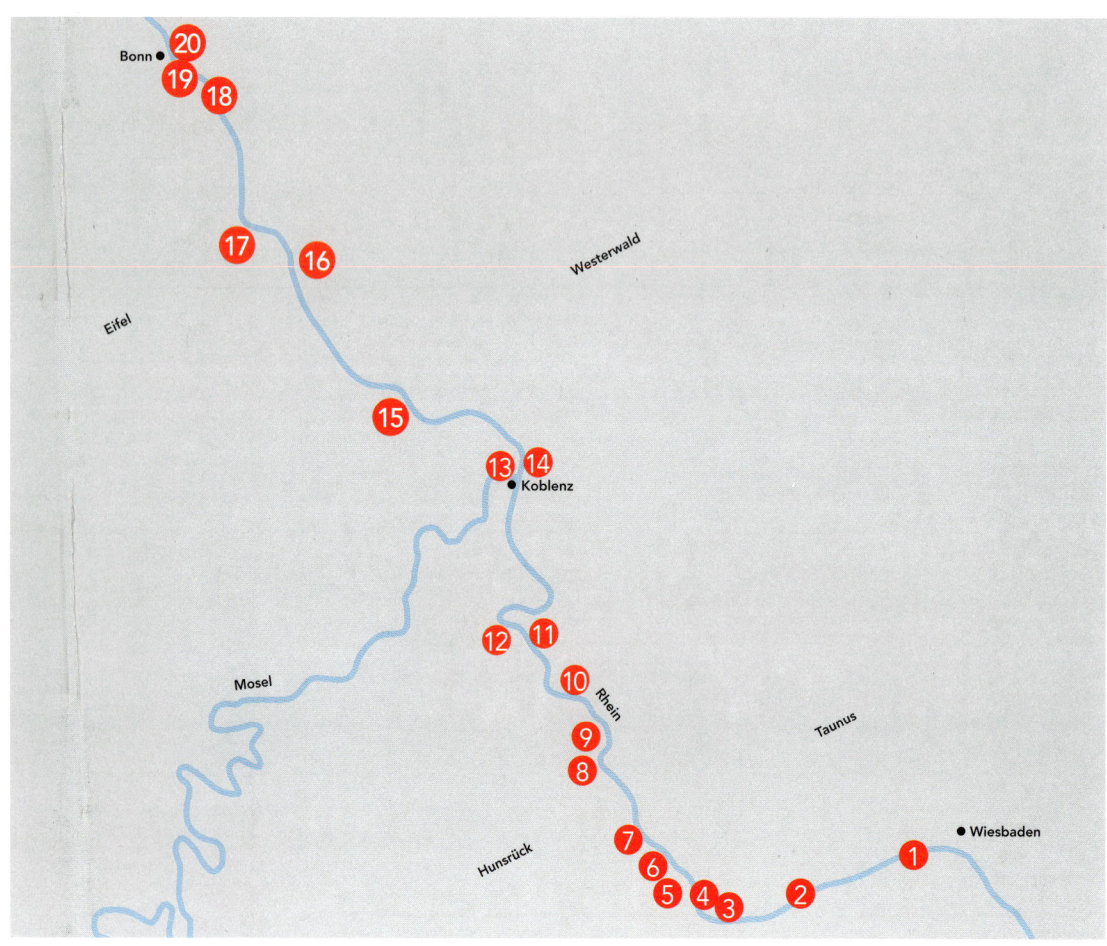

1. Eltville – *Eberbach Monastery*
2. Oestrich-Winkel – *Brentanohaus*
3. Rüdesheim – *Niederwald Gondola Lift*
4. Rüdesheim – *Niederwald Monument*
5. Trechtinsghausen – *Rheinstein Castle*
6. Rheindiebach – *Fürstenberg Castle Ruins*
7. Bacharach – *View down to Bacharach*
8. Oberwesel – *Günderodehaus*
9. Urbar – *Maria Ruh*
10. St. Goar – *Rheinfels Castle*
11. Kamp-Bornhofen – *"The Hostile Brothers"*
12. Boppard – *Gedeonseck*
13. Koblenz – *Deutsches Eck*
14. Koblenz – *Festung Ehrenbreitstein*
15. Andernach – *City Castle*
16. Linz – *Castle Square*
17. Remagen – *Rolandsbogen*
18. Königswinter – *Church St. Remigius*
19. Bonn – *Market Place*
20. Bonn – *Rheinaue*

The Rhine travels a distance of 1,324 km. Its origin lies in the transition area between the eastern and western Alps in Switzerland. The river is largely divided into 4 sections: the High Rhine begins at the spring and continues on to Basel. The next section, the Upper Rhine, ends in Bingen. There, after having travelled 500 km from the origin, the Middle Rhine spans the 155 km to Bonn. The final section leads from Bonn to the estuary and is called the Lower Rhine. The 30 km long northernmost part of the Upper Rhine is called the Rheingau. It begins in Wiesbaden and ends in Rüdesheim near Bingen. This book traces the Rhine as it travels through the Rheingau and the Middle Rhine region, both of which are among the most beautiful sections of the river.

In 1803, poet Heinrich von Kleist wrote: "He breaks through and the rocks give way, watching from above with amazement and admiration." He used these poignant words to express his enthusiasm for the Rhine gorges in the slate mountains. Heinrich von Kleist was not the only one enthralled by the river. For millennia, people settled here and created a unique cultural landscape. Farms, villages, towns, monasteries and castles were built along the wooded flanks of the Taunus and in the foothills of the fabled Siebengebirge. Droves of tourists from around the globe travel to the Rheingau and Middle Rhine Valley today. Among the most popular attractions are of course the castles, palaces and ruins – as well as the excellent wine. Nowhere in the world travellers can tour more historic fortifications in a comparably small region. In the early 19th century most of these impressive structures had crumbled, however, they provided the inspiration for the upcoming Rhine romanticism. Driven by cultural responsibility and to accommodate the increase in tourism the rebuilding of the ruins began in many places in the 19th century. Besides carefully restored historical monuments evolved contemporary architecture– among them the picturesque Stolzenfels Palace and Rheinstein Castle. Many castles and chateaus are now open for tours. The settlements in the region, some of which date back to the Stone Age, have their roots in the utilisation of the Rhine as a key trading and transportation route. The Celts settled in the Rheingau since prehistoric times, followed by Romans and Prince-electors, who all left behind world-famous buildings and art monuments. Quite a few of the resonant village and town names have Celtic or Roman origins. The communities often look back on 2,000 years of history. The basic structures of these buildings, which are often centuries old are therefore given lots of tender loving care.

The Romans also brought the wine to the Rhine. As of the 6th century, during the Franconian era, vineyards were cultivated on a large scale. In the centuries that followed, the terraces that Upper Middle Rhine Valley and Rheingau are famous for were designed. In these man-made optimized appellations winemakers are still harvesting grapes that produce wines coveted all over the world. The slate and volcanic ash soil as well as the gentle climate provide optimum conditions for e. g. Riesling, Pinot noir and Kerner grapes. The sun heats the soil throughout the day and keeps the vines warm overnight. Wineries, winemaker's properties and impromptu restaurants called "Strausswirtschaften" beckon guests to wine tastings.

In the past, not only wine cultivation, but also fishing and ship transportation were welcome sources of income. Barges and freight vessels travelled hundreds of kilometres on the stream. In the mid 19th century, steamboats and the new railway began bringing travellers to Germany's most famous slate cliff – the legendary Loreley – still the topic of countless songs.

Numerous castles and custom stations watched that trade taxes were paid. Shallow spots and cliffs, especially those along Loreley and Binger Loch still pose great risks for vessels travelling the river. It was not until recent decades that modern technology took over the jobs of traditional pilots. Tourism now is economic factor no. 1 to the Middle Rhine. Castles, chateaus and cultural monuments, vineyards and forests, idyllic promenades and craggy cliffs create a spectacular landscape. The popular hiking trails such as Rheinsteig introduce breathtaking overlooks at virtually every turn. The hospitality of the hotels and guest houses in the picturesque villages beckon visitors to linger. Towns such as Wiesbaden, Koblenz and Bonn make history come alive to an unforgettable experience. Upper Middle Rhine Valley was first proposed to the UNESCO as a world heritage site in 1973. Thirty years later on June 28, 2002, it was added to the list.

The Rheingau is a landscape and culture gem. Where the Rhine has to bypass the natural obstacle of the Taunus in the west, it stretches along the right banks of the Rhine between Wiesbaden and Rüdesheim. While it is only 2–3 km of width, Rheingau is about 30 km long. Thanks to its unique weather and geological conditions, it is the home of world-famous Rieslings. Here, where the Rhine sometimes reaches its maximum width, the upcoming fogs in the fall called "Traubendrücker" (grape pressers) foster the development of noble rot, thus creating what it takes to make the coveted Rheingau selections. While Rheingau is among Germany's smallest appellations, it looks back on a proud history. About 3,000 hectares of vineyards cover the sun-drenched southern slopes. The landscapes around them have diverse scenery.

Eberbach Monastery

Eberbach Monastery, a former Cistercian abbey on the fringes of Eltville built in 1136 by Bernhard of Clairvaux is one of the most beautiful and impressive monuments of mediaeval cloister construction. Originally inhabited by an abbot and 12 monks, Eberbach Monastery soon evolved into one of Germany's most prominent convents.

Over the centuries, wine cultivation was the central source of income. During the Middle Ages, the monastery established itself as the largest wine trader of its day time.

Eltville made its first appearance in official records in 1058. It is the oldest town in the Rheingau. The picturesque community presents fascinating monuments of its long history. In the idyllic alleys of the Old Town half-timbered houses dating back to the 16th–18th centuries are commonplace.

The 14th century electoral Stadtburg sits on the banks of the Rhine along with its tower and surrounding magnificent rose garden. The artfully built church Saint Peter and Paul's also hails from the 14th century. Even parts of the old town fortification are still intact today.

Some ancient noble mansions such as the Langwerther Hof, the Eltzer Hof and the Stockheimer Hof, which was first recorded to exist in 1363, have been fully preserved.

Johannes Gutenberg, who was banished from Mainz in 1462, subsequently lived at the Bechtermünzerhof for some time. Along with the proprietors, he set up a print shop here. From 1465–1467, the Latin work "Vocabularis ex quo" was printed here.

Eltville is nestled into prominent appellations dating back to the 12th century.

Island Eltviller Aue is located on the opposite bank of the Rhine.

Winemaker village Erbach in the north looks back on 1,000 years of history. It made a name for itself thanks to its excellent wines. Erbach's appellation "Marcobrunn" is acclaimed far and wide. The locally produced strawberries are also very popular.

Typical alley in Eltville

360° Panorama: Eltville – Eberbach Monastery ①

In the late 15th century cloister rooms such as the fraternity, which is now the cabinet cellar, and the lay refectory had to make room for the growing wine cultivation. The lay refectory now houses twelve historic wine presses. As secularisation progressed in the early 19th century, the monastic operations were ceased, while wine cultivation continued.

The monastery is now a venue for renowned events. It provided the backdrop for numerous scenes in the movie version of Umberto Eco's literary classic "The Name of the Rose". The monks originally used the 13th century former fraternity to perform domestic duties and spend idle hours that were part of monastic life.

After the Rheingau farmers' revolt of the early 16th century, which included the looting of numerous locations, the fraternity and the lay refectory were converted into wine cellars. The monks bricked up the windows to protect the precious wines from thieves. The monastery also housed the Large Barrel, then considered the 8th Wonder of the World thanks to its capacity of about 71,000 litres. However, it soon began to fall apart.

As of the early 18th century, the monks began to store especially rare wines in the former fraternity and called the vault the Cabinet Cellar. It was the cloister's treasure chest.

The first Cabinet wine label dates back to those days. The quality rating "Cabinet", which is now incorporated into the Wine Act and appreciated around the world, is based on this label.

Top: Cabinet Cellar; bottom: Cloister

Attractive Reinhartshausen Palace in the vicinity of Eltville was originally the domicile of the Knights at Erbach. It was torn down in 1801. Marianne of Prussia acquired the property in 1855 and built the current chateau. The palace underwent a conversion from 1987 to 1991 and is now a first class hotel.

Walluf to the south of Eltville is known for its wine cultivation and for the storks that breed in the bordering Nature Preserve.

Budenheim across the Rhine also produces excellent wines. However, the town is primarily known for the 1911 discovery of the fossil remains of a 20-million-year-old rhinoceros now on exhibit in the museum Senckenberg in Frankfurt am Main.

Neighbouring Heidesheim is acclaimed for its wine cultivation, the St. Georg's Chapel dating back to 650, the 1150 Windeck Castle and the palace mill.

Crass Castle, which dates back to the 11th century, is now a hotel.

Crass Castle

Prince-elector's castle with rose garden

OESTRICH-WINKEL

Brentanohaus

Oestrich-Winkel is a famous vinemaker village with numerous excellent appellations and a long history. A mine dating back to the Bronze Age was found in Winkel. The famous "Graue Haus" (Grey House) probably dates back to the 11th century. Oestrich is characterised by its attractive half-timbered 17th/18th century houses. The wine loading crane completed in 1745, which was used through 1926, is the town's distinctive landmark. The Mittelheim district is home to the magnification Saint Aegidius Basilica built from 1118 to 1131.

In 1751, Johann Michael Ackermann built an impressive structure in Winkel. In 1804 it was acquired by the noble Brentano family as a summer residence. The Brentano House hosted many famous guests, including the Brothers Grimm, Frederick Charles of Savigny and the Baron of Stein, as well as Johann Wolfgang von Goethe. The room occupied by the poet during his Rhine travels from 1814 to 1815 can be viewed today – in the original style of Goethe's day and age. Goethe enjoyed the "Eilfer," an 1811 vintage of the appellation so much that it inspired him to write works such as the "Sankt-Rochus-Fest zu Bingen" and "Im Rheingau Herbsttage".

Vollrads, a 13th century palace, is nestled into the appellations three kilometres north of Oestrich-Winkel. Built in the 15th century, the distinctive residential tower is still intact. The manor house was added in 1684. Numerous additions complemented the property over the centuries. Vollrads Chateau is known for the select wines cultivated in the bordering vineyards and now provides a romantic backdrop for music events and wine tastings. It also houses a first class restaurant.

Schwarzenstein Castle is located north east of Vollrads Chateau just above Johannisberg. Its tower and pinnacles give it a mediaeval appearance; however it was not built until 1873. Surrounded by a park it now houses a hotel and restaurant.

Vollrads Chateau

360° Panorama Oestrich-Winkel – Brentanohaus ❷

Hattenheim is a small yet history-laden community in the Rheingau. Probably already settled in the early Stone Age, it boasts one of the Rheingau's premium appellations. Hattenheim Castle was established around 1118 and is now a popular venue for events. Hattenheim also possesses one of the most beautiful wine tasting stands at an idyllic spot right on the banks of the Rhine. Rhine island Marianen Aue spreads in the water fronting Hattenheim.

Ingelheim on the left side of the Rhine across from the Marianen Aue calls itself "the City of Red Wine" and was settled in prehistoric times. The town acquired prominence under Charlemagne who set up a Palatinate here. The local museum provides insights into this era.

Ingelheim's famous red wine festival takes place annually on the last weekend in September and draws multitudinous visitors. The town also boasts numerous other historic buildings, such as the Saalkirche (a church) from 997, the church Saint Remigius from 1739, the 12th century castle church, the church Saint Michael from 1721, the Bismarck tower, the Ohrenbrücken gate and the Malakoff tower.

Geisenheim made its first appearance in records in 772. It is home to the 19th century "Villa Monrepos" built by the founder of the famous research institution for wine and garden cultivation, Eduard von Lade.

A 700-year-old linden tree towers over the town centre of the "Linden town." The magnificent 16th century Church of the Holy Cross, also called the "Rheingauer Dom" (Rheingau cathedral) overlooks the vast settlement.

Geisenheim was one of the stations in the Rheingau, where passing ships had to pay duties as of the end of the 12th century. The tender for payment was a spice that was highly valued back then – pepper. This was the invention of the term "Pfefferzoll" (pepper toll). The 1618 customs house in Old Town is still intact.

Schönborn Chateau, which dates back to 1550 is still in the possession of the family Schönborn and nestled into a vineyard.

The famous pilgrimage destination of Marienthal is not far from Geisenheim. The church was first sanctified in 1330; the world's first monastic print shop opened in 1468. Hansenberg Chateau sits on a mountain of the same name. In 1824 it was originally built as an orphanage. In 2003 it was converted into a school and boarding school for highly intelligent students.

Impressions of Hattenheim   *Flea market in Geisenheim*

Johannisberg Chateau, which is nestled into 35 hectares of vineyards near Geisenheim, is one of the traditional wineries of the Rheingau. Wine cultivation on the Johannisberg began as early as 817; the construction of the building was initiated in the 12th century. Its famous Johannisberg Riesling, however, had to be attributed to the Fulda Abbey, which commissioned the construction of the palace on the foundation of a former Benedictine monastery and planted Riesling vines in the appellations.

Also the start of the grape harvest had to be approved by the Abbot of Fulda every year and a messenger was sent to get his consent. In 1775 the courier returned so tardily that the grapes had begun to rut. The result was surprising as the wine produced was of a new quality not known before, producing classics such as the „Auslese", „Beerenauslese", „Trockenbeerenauslese" and ice wine. Connoisseurs can thank the courier who made Johannisberg Chateau history as the late arriving horseman.

The Johannisberg and the building had to live through many changes in proprietorship. The wines continue to mature in the traditional manner in wooden barrels in the expansive cellars. The premium sparkling wine produced here is called "Fürst von Metternich" – in honour of the former Austrian Foreign Minister Klemens von Metternich, who was in charge of the property as of 1816.

The evolution of Johannisberg, the historic winemaker town, is closely linked to the former Benedictine monastery. The story of the craftsmen who settled here alongside the winemakers over the course of the centuries is still evident in some old mills.

Residents have been committed to the cultivation of magnificent roses for decades, which now characterise the unique townscape. The festival of roses and wine takes place every year in September.

Johannisberg Chateau

RÜDESHEIM

Niederwald Gondola Lift

The small winemaker town of Rüdesheim and its one-of-a-kind village centre are definitely outstanding symbols of Rhine romanticism. This is where Rheingau style terraces meld with the narrow valley of the Rhine. Originally built in the style of a Franconian scattered village, Rüdesheim first appears in records of 1074. Even then wine was cultivated here. Numerous historic building monuments are still intact. Castle Brömserburg, also called "Niederburg", probably built in the first millennium is on the list of UNESCO world heritage sites along with the Upper Middle Rhine Valley. Close by is the 10th/11th century Boosenburg, the former "Oberburg", the upper castle. Only the tower remains of the original castle. Among the other sights are the Brömser Hof, 14th century Catholic church Saint Jacob, the Adlerturm and the Mediaeval Torture Museum.

Without a doubt, the Drosselgasse is the most famous historic alley. Originally a favourite quarter for ship operators on the Rhine, guest houses sprang up all around. The Drosselhof, built in 1727, is the oldest wine house. Restaurants and cafés that line the narrow alley literally compete for your attention with their culinary delights.

Eibingen Abbey (Saint Hildegard's Abbey) is located in the Eibingen district of Rüdesheim. The monastery, which was built from 1900 to 1904, is dominated by the imposing new Roman double tower of the abbey church. The structures sprang from the Benedictine abbey of Eibingen founded here in 1165 by famous Hildegard of Bingen.

The Drosselhof in the Drosselgasse

360°Panorama: Rüdesheim – Niederwald Gondola Lift **3**

Mediaeval festival in Rüdesheim

Vineyards near Rüdesheim

RÜDESHEIM

Niederwald Monument

More than 38 m tall, the Niederwalddenkmal perched above Rüdesheim and its giant "Germania" statue stand as the symbol of the unity of the German Empire that can be seen from afar. In 1871, Wilhelm I's Emperor's Proclamation sealed the victory over France and the political union of Germany. The foundation stone of the monument was laid in 1877. It was built based on the design of Karl Weißbach by Johannes Schilling and unveiled under the auspices of the Emperor in 1883.

The 12.5 m tall Germania statue was to symbolise the "Watch of the Rhine" and commemorate the foundation of the new German state. Since then it has been a tourist magnet. The monument is located inside the enthralling Niederwald landscape park. At the foot of the monument one can enjoy fantastic panoramic views of the surrounding appellations.

The 13th century Ehrenfels castle ruins are just a short distance from the monument. They boast 33 m tall corner towers and sit on the steep slopes of the Rüdesheim mountains.

Niederwald Monument

360° Panorama: Rüdesheim – Niederwald Monument **4**

Bingen is situated on the estuary of Rhine and Nahe. Its earliest roots date back to the Celtic era. The Romans and Franconians, archbishops and the Prussians arrived later.

Visitors have the opportunity to view uncovered remains of a Roman farm dating back to the first centuries AD at the "Villa Rustica" in Bingen forest. Among the most famous sights are the 15th century Saint Martin's Basilica; the chapel Saint Roch, which was set up in the location of two preceding buildings from 1893 to 1895, and the ancient 15th century crane.

Klopp Castle built in the 13th century sits atop of the Kloppberg. Rupertsberg gained fame thanks to Saint Hildegard of Bingen who founded her first convent here in honour of Saint Rupert. It was blown up in 1857 to make room for a railway trail.

Bingen's most famous landmark is the Mäuseturm (the Mouse Tower of Bingen) on a small Rhine island originally built as a customs office in the 14th century. The new gothic tower built from 1856 to 1858 took its place. The 11th century Drusus Bridge is considered Germany's oldest stone bridge and spans the 126 m wide Nahe just before it merges with the Rhine and connects Bingen with its district Bingerbrück.

Top: Saint Martin's Basilica; bottom: View of Bingen

Top: Binger Loch with Mäuseturm; bottom: Chapel Saint Roch

The romantic red wine village Assmannshausen was suburbanised by Rüdesheim in 1977 and is especially well-know for its premium red wine. It first appeared in records in 1108 under the name "Hasemannshusen." The still partially intact ring wall on the Rhine end was erected to protect the town from enemies and ice movements. A most amazing sight is the 14th century Catholic parish church Holy Cross.

Magnificent half-timbered houses can be found in Assmannshausen. Some of them house romantic restaurant, where connoisseurs can taste excellent Pinot noir wines from the "Höllenberg" appellation.

Old Town of Assmannshausen

Top: "Höllenberg" appellation; bottom: Assmannshausen and Rheinstein Castle

Rheinstein Castle and Reichenstein Castle

Located on the left-hand bank of the Rhine, winemaker town Trechtingshausen, which has been suburbanised by Bacharach, has been on the UNESCO list of world cultural heritage sites as part of the Middle Rhine since 2003. The town was first mentioned in records in 1122; however, it is safe to assume that it was settled even in Roman times. Old rows of gravesites also provide evidence of Franconian settlements.

Reichenstein Castle dates back to the 11th/12th centuries. It was rebuilt after having been destructed numerous times, however, as of the 16th century it was left to deteriorate. The ruins were blown up in 1689. Baron Nikolaus of Kirsch-Puricelli rebuilt it into its current condition from 1899 to 1902 based on the new gothic residential castle plans in English style drawn up by architect Strebel.

Clemens Chapel sits on the banks of the Rhine just below Reichenstein Castle. It is a late Roman pillar basilica. Discoveries indicate that it has origins as far back as the 4th century, albeit the current structure was probably not built until the early 13th century. The chapel houses graves of the 15th and 17th centuries

Rheinstein Castle with its fabulous appearance is proudly perched atop its cliff near Trechtingshausen. Likely established in the 14th century by the Archbishopric of Mainz, the castle began crumbling after a tumultuous history as of the end of the 16th century. The ruins were acquired by Prince Frederick of Prussia in 1823. He commissioned its reconstruction to match the romantic Rhine style of the 19th century, making it one of the first previously destroyed Rhine castles to be rebuilt. The castle has been a privately owned property since 1975. Its festive and intricately restored rooms are available for weddings or celebrations of all kinds. Today's knight's hall was completed between 1827 and 1829. Some of the precious coloured glass windows date back to the 16th century, others were reproduced in the 19th century. The magnificent wall frescos and the elegant furnishings further enhance the fascinating ambience.

Rheinstein Castle

360° Panorama: Trechtinghausen – Rheinstein Castle ⑤

Rheinstein Castle

Vineyard near Hallgarten

Fürstenberg Castle Ruins

Winemaker town Rheindiebach first appears in records of 1461 under the name "Niederdieppach." Slopes on which Riesling vines are being cultivated surround the village and offer fantastic views. Gothic church Saint Mauritius, which dates back to the 13th century, awaits visitors with impressive frescos in Oberdiebach. Remnants of the former gothic town fortification and the so-called "Halbe Turm" (Half Tower) can be admired in Rheindiebach. The ruins of Fürstenberg sit on a cliff proudly overlooking Rheindiebach. Former Fürstenberg Castle was built by order of Engelbert I of Berg, Archbishop of Cologne, from 1219 to 1220. The French destroyed it in 1689; since 1993 the ruins have been undergoing careful reconstruction.

Just above Niederheimbach and a few kilometres from Rheindiebach up the river you will find the defence fortress Heimburg, which was erected as a stronghold against the Palatinate earls between 1296 and 1305. Later used as an official residence, it burned out in 1639. Its reconstruction began in the 19th century; today it has been restored to a new splendour thanks to its current owner.

Sooneck Castle south of Rheindiebach is considered one of the most typical knights' castles on the Middle Rhine. During the 13th century the reeves of Kornelimünster Abbey used it as a robber barons' stronghold under the name "Saneck." In 1282 it was destroyed by King Rudolph of Habsburg. Frederick William IV had the ruins transformed into a hunting castle post 1843. Thanks to its imposing location and appearance as well as its enthralling interior the castle is a tourist magnet.

Sooneck Castle

360° Panorama: Rheindiebach, Fürstenberg Castle Ruins 6

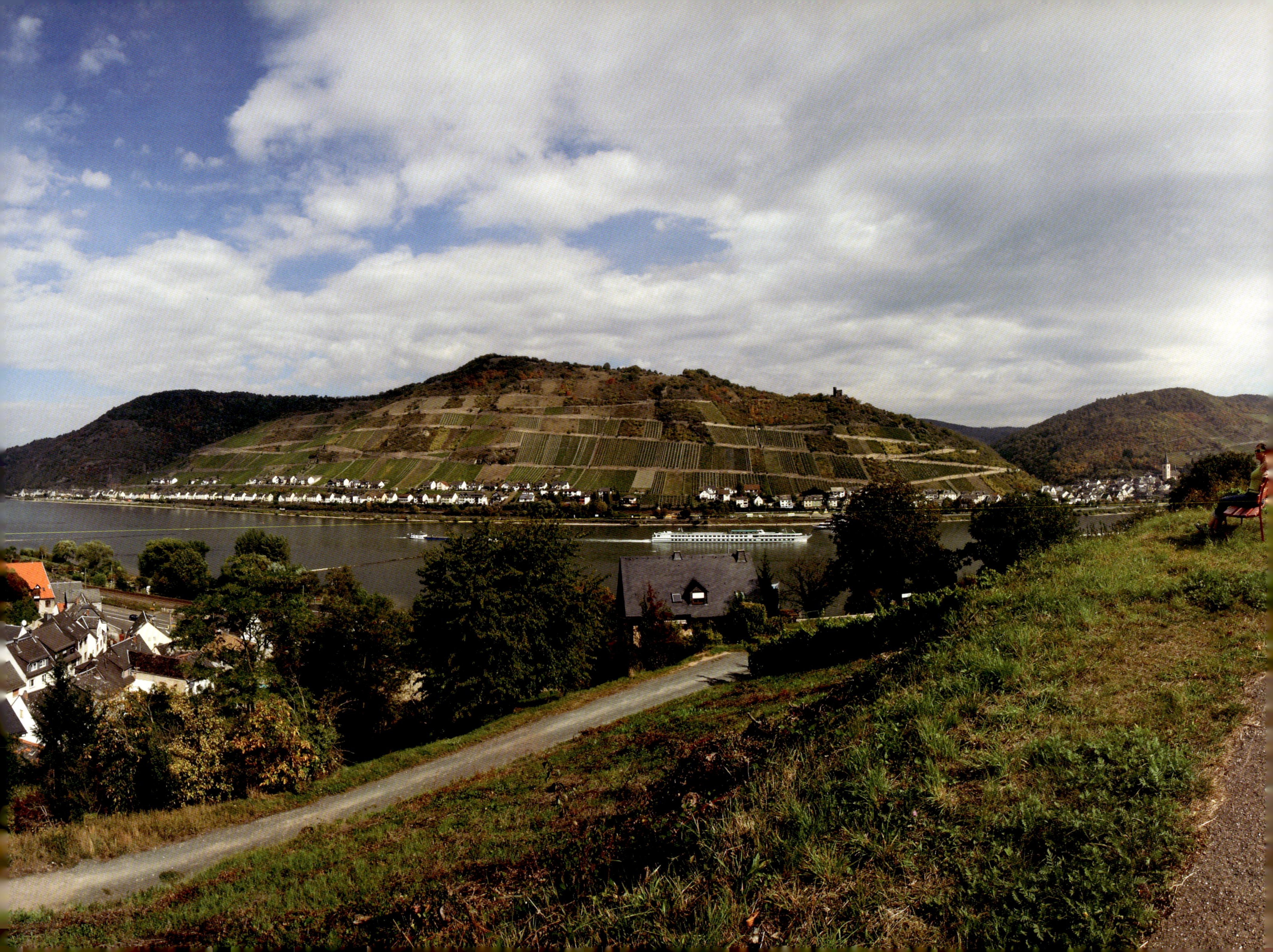

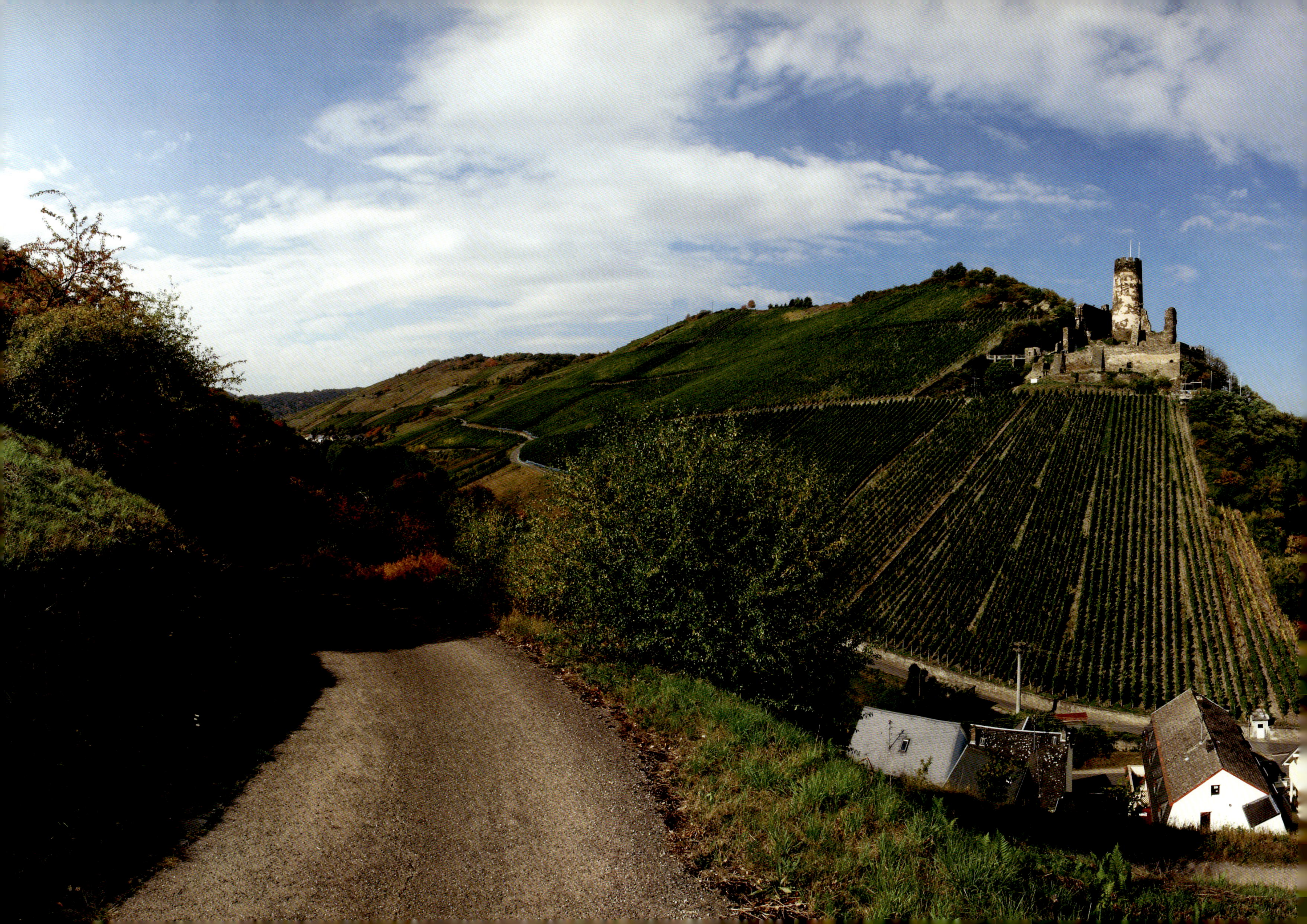

Lorch, a town sitting right on the Wisper estuary, is one of the Rhine romance highlights. The small winemaker town made its first documented appearance in 1085 and draws droves of tourists thanks to its historic alleys. Catholic parish church Saint Martin, which dates back to the 13th century and boasts a 1483 high altar, is considered an eminent art history monument. Others sights include a 1527 fortification tower, the mediaeval Witches' Tower and the 16th century "Hilchenhaus", which is due for renovation. The Nollig ruins are perched above Lorch. The structure was erected as a watchtower in the early 14th century. The terrain surrounding the ruins is considered one of Hesse's most diverse habitats for animals and plants otherwise only found in Southern Europe. The large Saint Bonifatius Church built in new gothic style from 1877 to 1879 towers over Lorch's district Lorchhausen, which established its place in history in 1211 under the name "Husen." The Lorcher Werth, a Nature Preserve, can be found between Lorch and Niederheimbach. It consists of two islands in the centre of the Rhine connected by a dam.

View of Lorchhausen

Lorch and parish church Saint Martin

Kaub, also called the "Blücherstadt", was first mentioned in records of 983 under the name "Cuba villula". In the 14th century the town evolved into a key customs point and acquired town rights. Even today, remnants of the historic town fortification, including five main towers, remain intact. Picturesque Zollstrasse, the old customers' houses and office of 1552, document the history of the station. To prevent passers-by from skipping a stop at the Kaub customs' point, the Palatinate earls erected Pfalzgrafenstein Castle on a rock island upstream from the town in the 14th century. Customs' officers worked here through 1867. In the city centre of Kaub visitors will be enthralled by numerous other remarkable sights, such as 14th/15th century church Saint Trinitatis, Saint Nicholas built from 1770 to 1772, and just a few steps from it the Old Town Hall, a 1655–1663 reproduction of the burned down original building of 1603.

Gutenfels Castle is perched on top of a cliff to the north east of Kaub. It was built in the first half of the 13th century and restored in the late 19th century. Today it is operated as a hotel.

In 1813/1814 Kaub was made its mark as an important venue in German history. Field Marshal von Blücher and his troops crossed the Rhine from here and embarked on their battle against the French during the Prussian Liberation War; putting an end to French occupation. A monument in his honour was erected on the banks of the Rhine at the end of the 19th century. Blücher Museum located in the Metzgergasse is well worth a visit.

The bridge heads installed by the allied forces after World War I on the right side of the Rhine left an unoccupied area shaped like a bottleneck due to an error. In 1919 the Free State Bottleneck evolved in this spot between Kaub and Lorch. About 8,000 residents lived in this enclave prospering with smuggled goods and Free State money, which had been created just for this area and is worth a lot for collectors today. Overnight, wine from the occupied Rheingau was smuggled into the Free State on ox carts to protect them from consumption by the occupying soldiers. These wines now fetch top bids among connoisseurs. It was not until 1923 that the Free State was conquered by French troops and dissolved.

Pfalzgrafenstein Castle

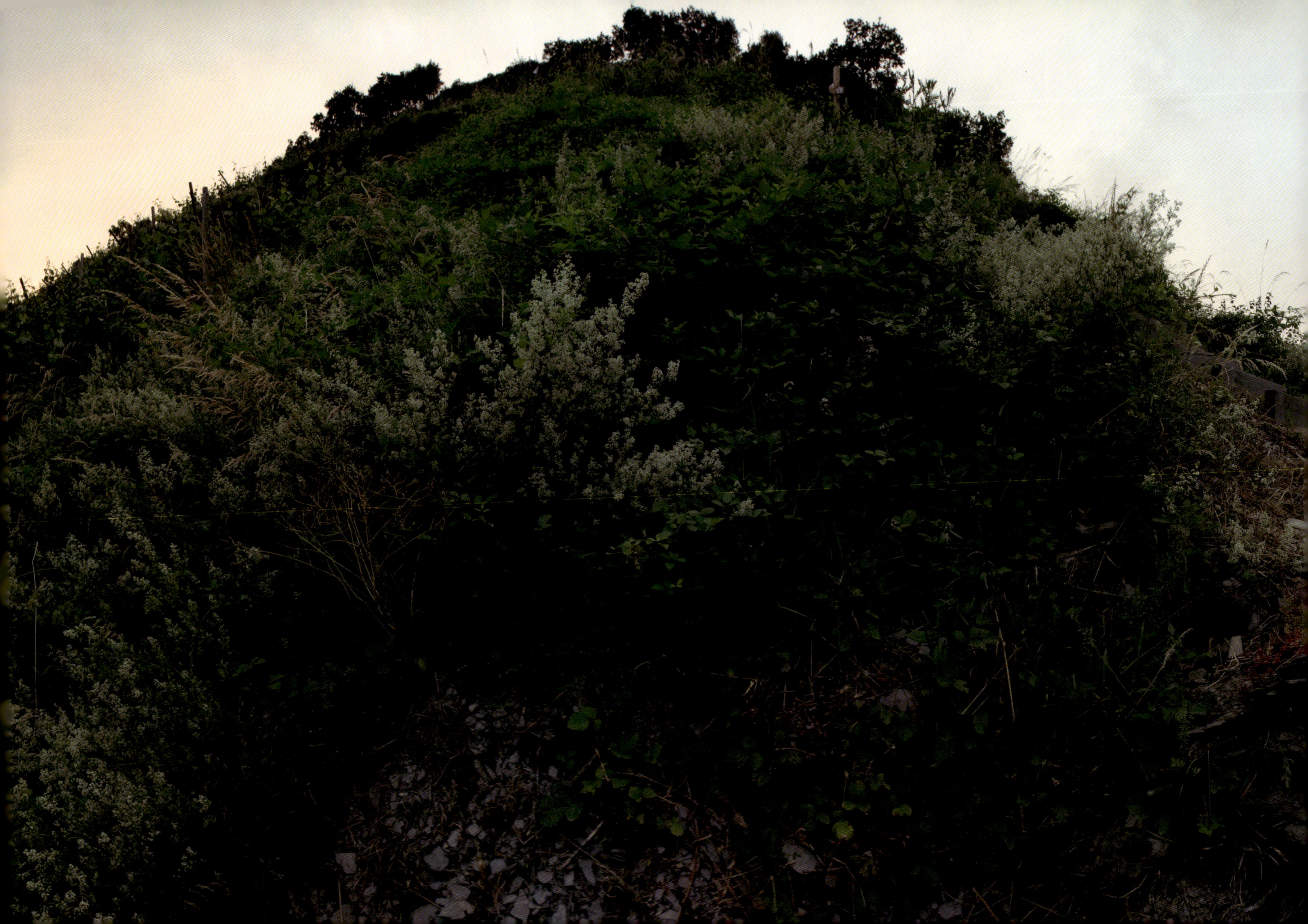

Stahleck Castle

It is easy to understand why the beauty of Bacharach made such an impression on writers such as Heinrich Heine and Victor Hugo – just a glance at the romantic winemaker town will do it. Its original name "Baccaracus" indicates its Celtic origins.

The town has likely been a consistent settlement since the Franconian era; it is first mentioned in records of 1019.

History books make references to Stahleck Castle just a short time later – in 1102. Today, the castle is a youth hostel. In the 12th century it was a residence of the Palatinate Earls bei Rhein and was destroyed during the Palatinate Succession War. It was rebuilt in the 20th century. In 1214 the Palatinate and the town of Bacharach were passed to the House of Wittelsbach.

In subsequent years, Bacharach prospered as a wine trading centre. Prussia seized the town in 1814. Today it enthrals visitors with its wealth of sights. Parts of the old town wall, as well as a few towers and many other interesting old buildings are still intact. Bacharach boasts famous appellations such as the "Bacharacher Posten" and the "Bacharacher Wolfshöhle".

Stahlberg Castle sits on a nose-shaped cliff in the Steeger Valley. It was likely erected by the Archbishopric of Cologne in the 12th century. Cologne's archbishop used it to safeguard his property and customs rights. The castle was destroyed in 1689. A distinctive round tower still overlooks the entrance area of the ruins with its shielding wall and ditch.

Stahleck Castle

360° Panorama: View down to Bacharach ❼

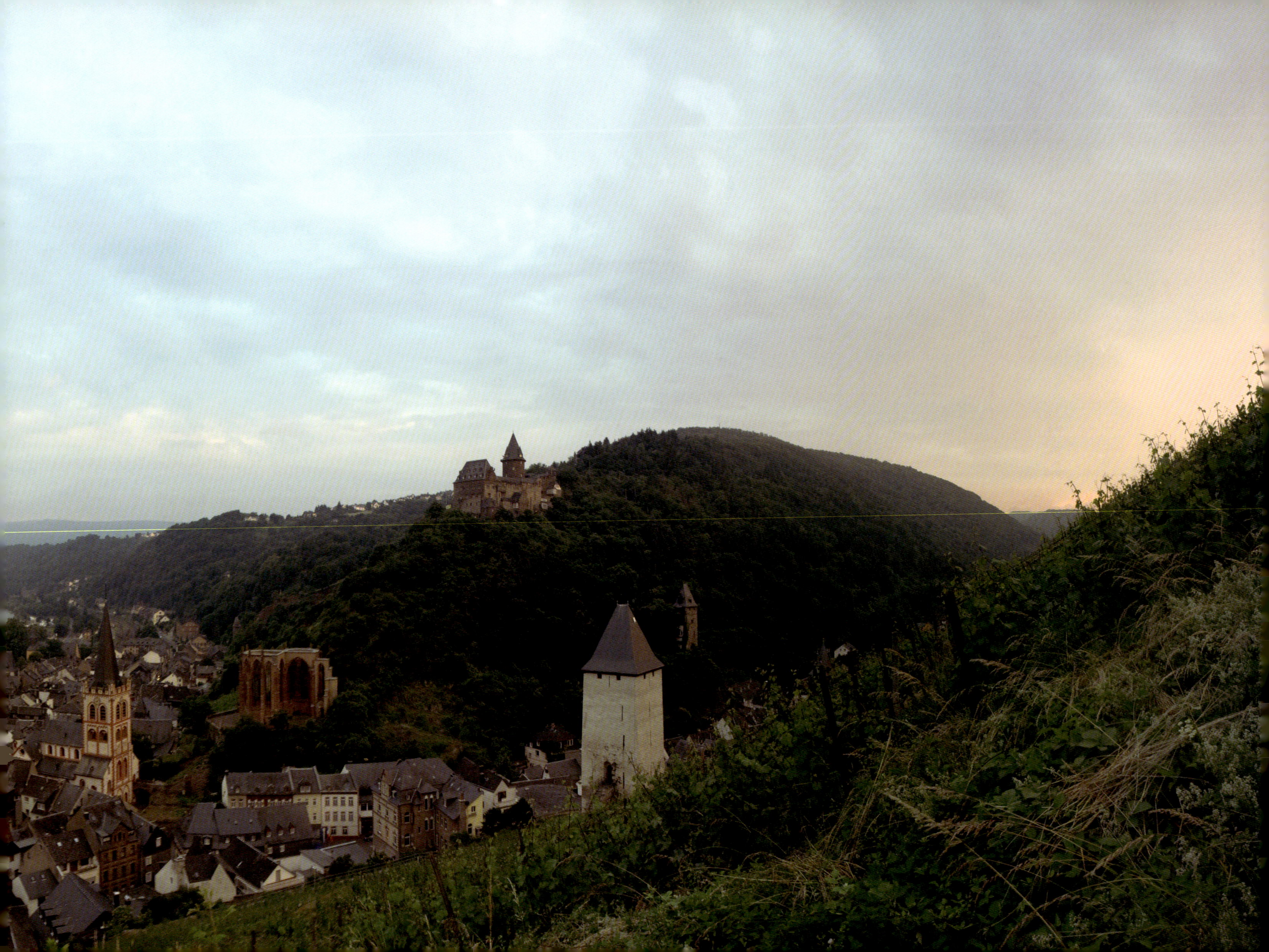

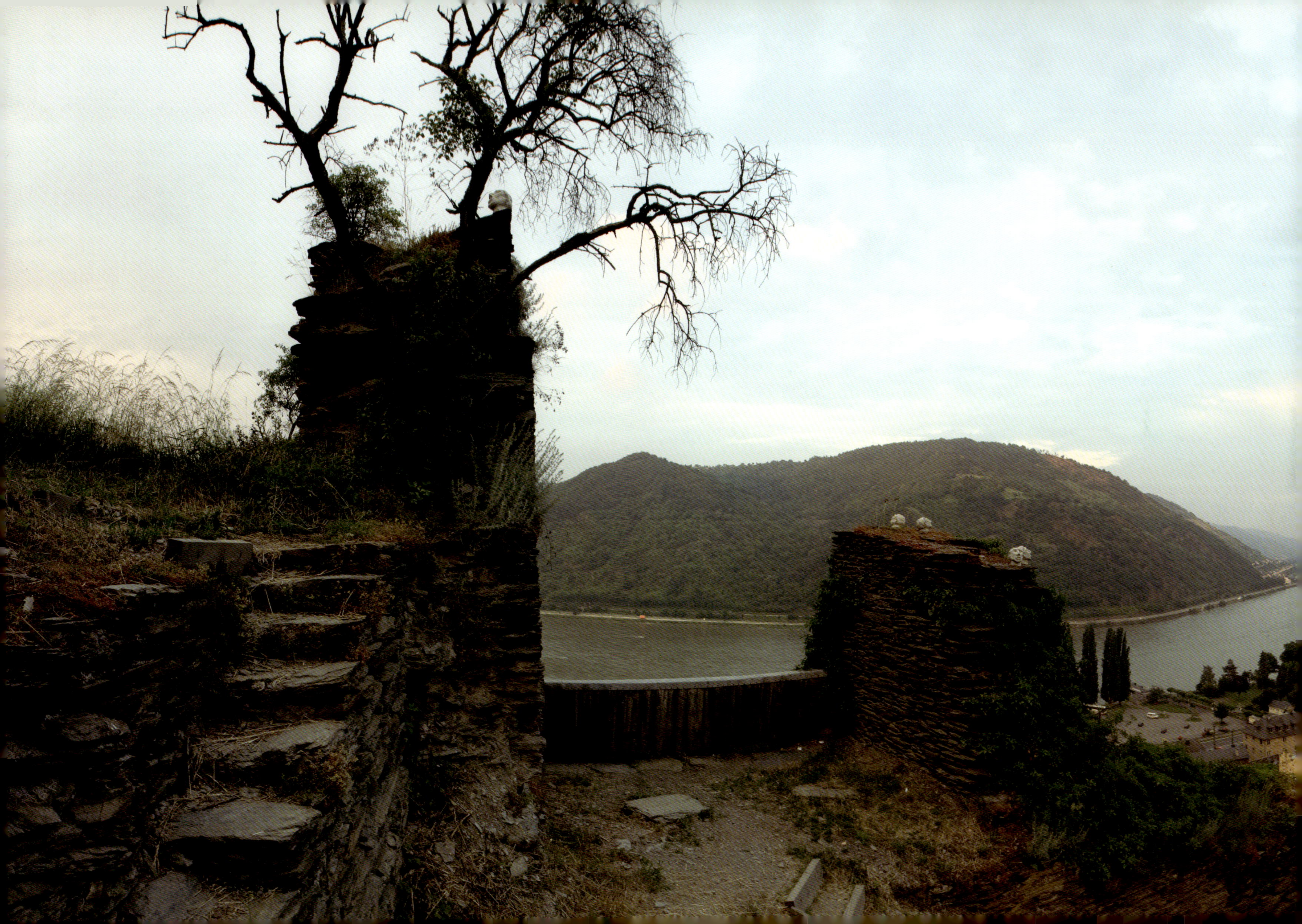

A group of well-maintained half-timbered houses embellish the Old Town of Bacharach. The most remarkable are the Old House of 1568, House Sickingen with its 1420 basement, House Utsch of the "Hunter of Palatinate" dating back to 1585, churches Saint Peter and Saint Nicholas and the ruins of the gothic 13th century Werner's Chapel.

A gem for every wine and nature enthusiast can be found in the middle of the Rhine just north of Bacharach: The small, uninhabited Rhine island Heyles'en Werth. Vines cover up the entire island. Locals frequently refer to the island as "the Werth". It was originally named for its former owner Hans Heylesen, who had been awarded legal property rights in 1593 by the then reigning Count Palatine.

Since 1797 the idyllic island has been part of the "Fritz Bastian Erbhof" winery, which is steeped in tradition. It is one of the most famous appellations of the region. While the 150 m wide and 680 m long island is a nature preserve, guests have the option to tour it with the owners for wine tastings.

Historic Old Town of Bacharach

Historic city centre of Bacharach

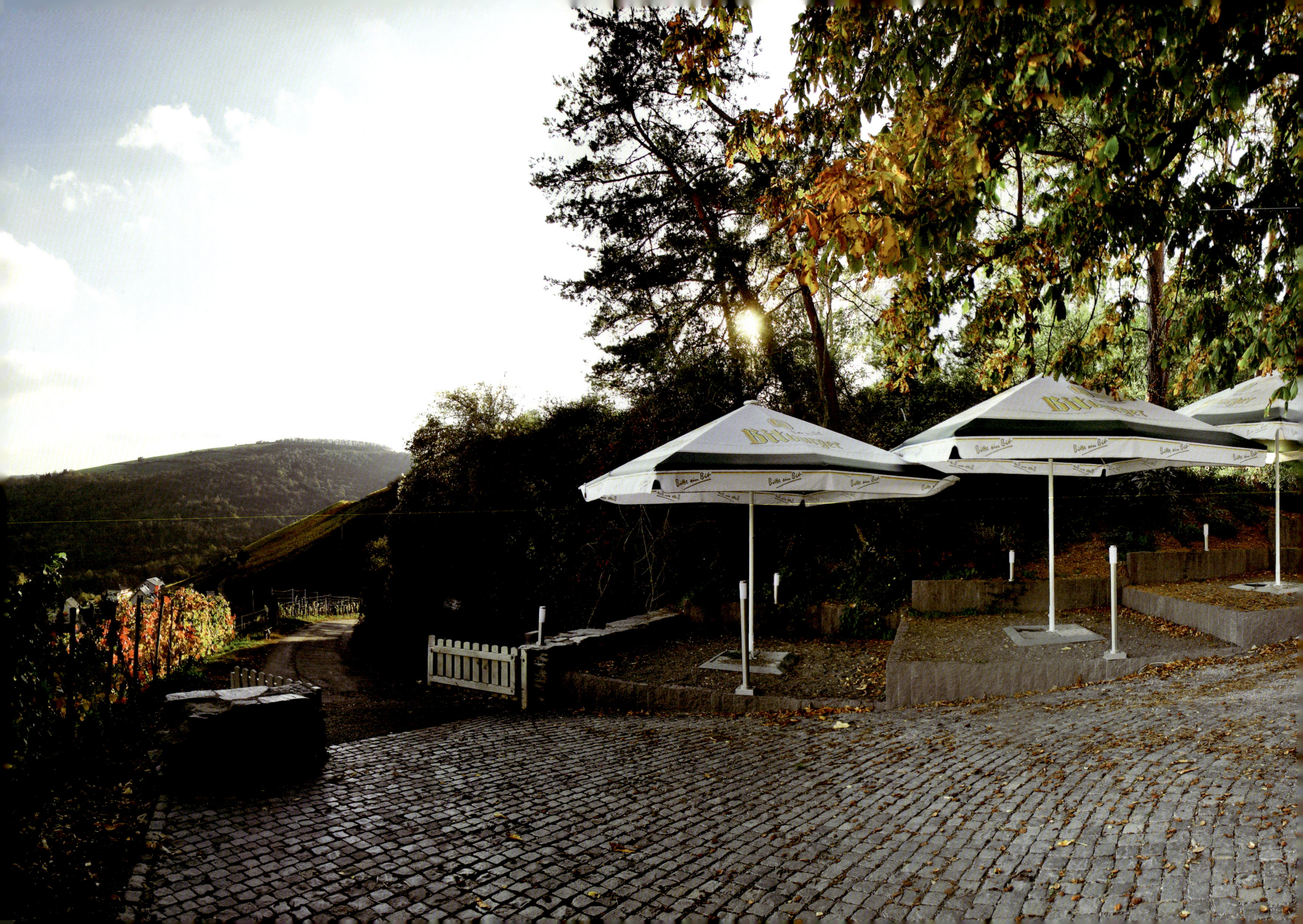
Bitburger
Bitte ein Bit

OBERWESEL

Schönburg Castle

Oberwesel on the western bank of the Rhine is probably of Celtic origin, its townscape with its well-preserved mediaeval appearance is one of Germany's most beautiful historic places. Oberwesel acquired free town rights as early as 1220. The construction of the town wall with its once 21 defence towers continued until the mid 14th century. Expansive ruins like impressive 16 towers including the imposing "Ochsenturm" survived the tumultuous history of the town. The gothic Liebfrauenkirche of 1309 houses mediaeval bells and a hand-carved golden altar which is unique in the Rhine region. Schönburg Castle, which was erected in the 12th century, and its 72 ha vineyard tower high above the roofs of the town. The property was once a typical Ganerben castle boasting three separate residential complexes and three donjons. It provided living quarters for multiple family lines of the Knights of Schonenberg. Destroyed by the French in 1689, it was rebuilt in the 20th century. Legend says that once upon a time seven beautiful sisters lived here. Numerous knights attempted to win the hearts of the virgins by winning competitions. None of them succeeded, and they besieged the castle. The sisters put on a feast and a drawing to decide who would become their husbands. As the winners arrived to pick up their brides, they did not find anyone but seven dolls made of straw. The virgins had long escaped taking boats down the Rhine, but they drowned. Seven rocks emerged from the Rhine and are known as "Die sieben Schwestern". The Tauber Werth, downstream from Oberwesel, is a small island just off the left bank of the Rhine. It is located near a shoal, and if the water level of the Rhine is low the island can be reached on foot.

Schönburg Castle

360° Panorama: View from the Siebenjungfrauenblick with the Günderodehaus down to Oberwesel ⑧

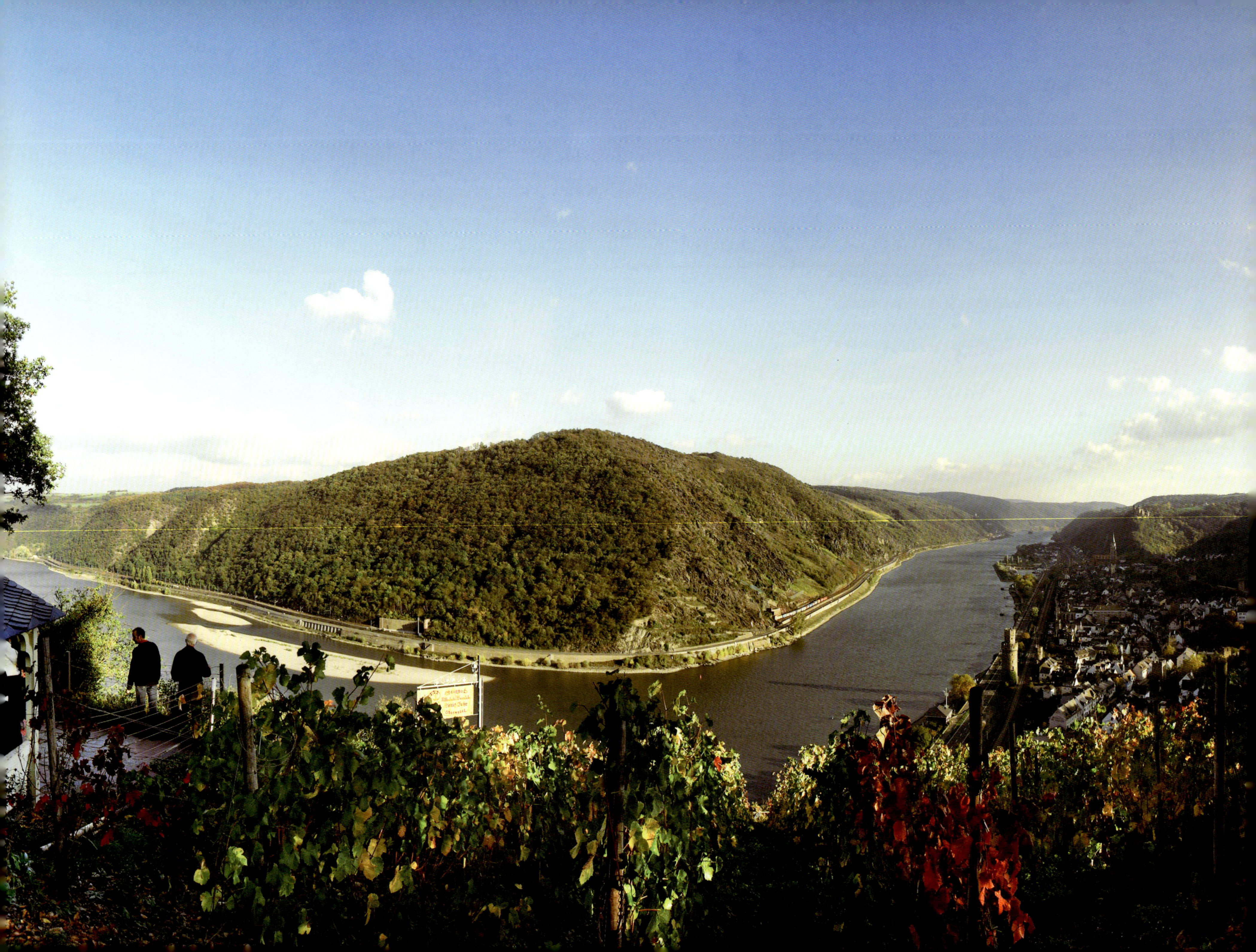

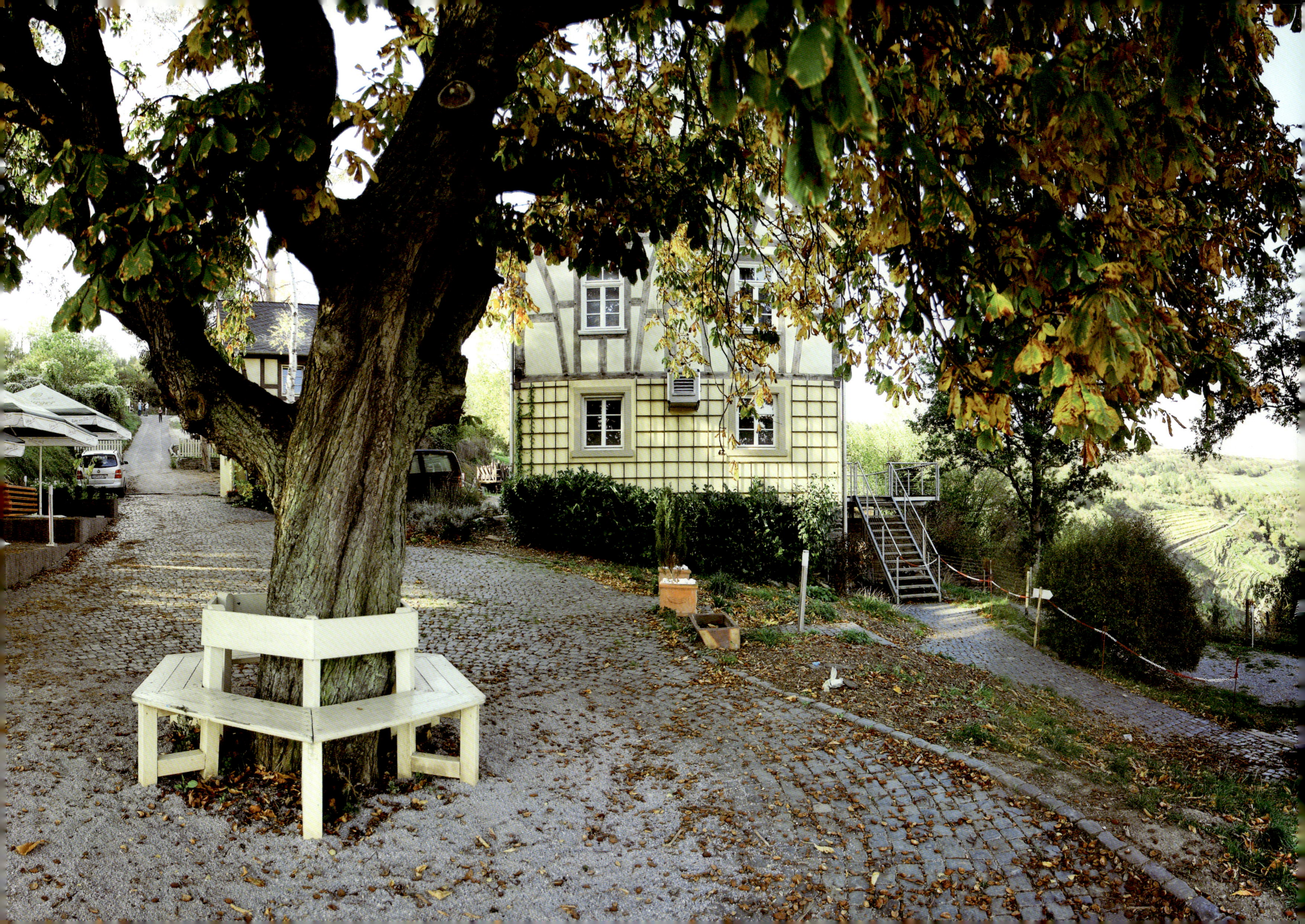

Town Hall in Oberwesel

Top: "Bemaltes Haus" (the Painted House); bottom: Hotel Römerkrug

The Rhine near Oberwesel

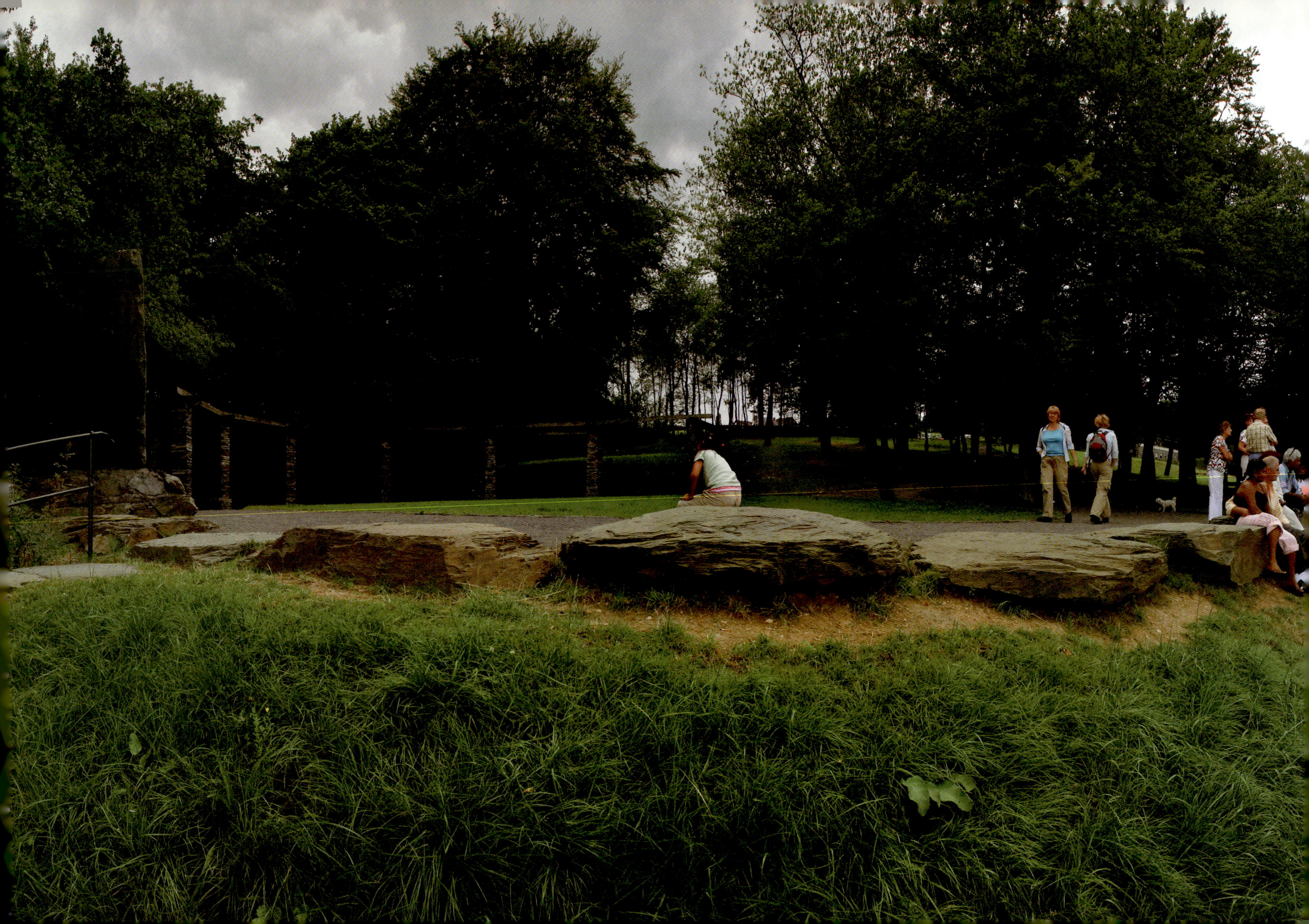

Maria Ruh

Few outlook points provide more imposing impressions of the Rhine and its surrounding sights than Maria Ruh just north of Oberwesel near Urbar. It offers unforgettable scenic views of the fabled Loreley cliff on the opposite side; deep into the narrowest point of the Rhine and downstream of Maus and Katz castles. At this point, the Rhine is only 113 m of width.

The idyllic high Rhine village of Urbar which was French two times places a lot of emphasis on hospitality. The small town and its 800 residents make every effort to offer their guests not only an enchanting vacation setting but great services along with numerous accommodations, including a well-maintained hotel. Sights here include the Catholic Saint Anthony's Church with its magnificent baroque altar which dates back to 1715, and the "Winzerhaus" which serves premium wines from the "Beulsberg" and "Ölsberg" appellations to satisfy more secular cravings.

The name "Maria Ruh" was probably derived from the special geographical conditions of the river route: On these dangerous Rhine kilometres it is located on the calm side of the river and is protected by Saint Mary – the patron saint of the mariners. On the other side is the enticing Loreley with its dangerous protracting slate cliff that reaches up from the water almost vertically.

Following a legend a beautiful girl named Loreley sat on the cliff in the evenings, combing her blond hair while singing enchanting melodies. This distracted many of mariners, causing them to steer their ships straight into the dangerous reefs, rocks and vortices.

A monument commemorating the three fathers of the famous Loreley song can be found on Maria Ruh. In 1801 Clemens Brentano's ballad "Zu Bacharach am Rhein" made the "Lore Lay" a classic of world literature. Heinrich Heine turned it into rhyming lyrics some 23 years later and Friedrich Silcher added a melodic tune in 1837.

An attractive park was landscaped around Maria Ruh in 2005.

View of the Loreley

360° Panorama: Urbar – Maria Ruh **9**

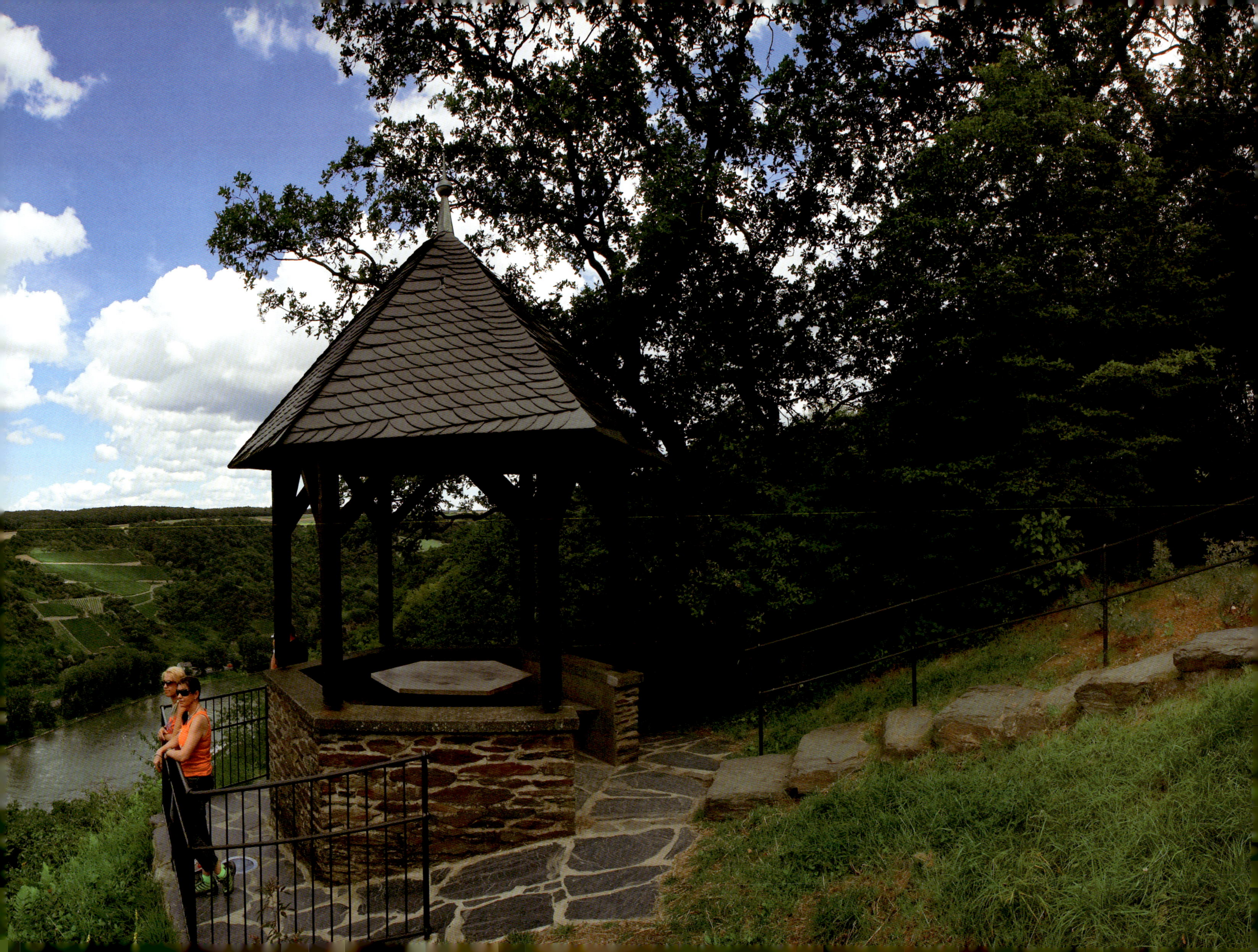

Maria Ruh

The name "Rheinsteig" which means Rhine Climb says it all: "Steig" refers to climbing. At the very latest during the "royal stage" between Kaub and St. Goarshausen everyone realizes what the term "Steig" refers to.

After leaving the forest and meadow land just below in the Urbach Valley, hikers now find themselves making their way up the craggy rocks to the Spitznack outlook with its rock pulpit. The climb up and down can easily be completed with the assistance of ropes.

The plateau offers an encounter with overwhelming beauty. If you have no fear of heights you can get all the way up to the front edge and stare down the drop of about 100 m. From the overlook pulpit, even hikers who are not quite as bold can enjoy magnificent views of the Loreley Cliff, which is only about a kilometre away, the attractive winemaker village Oberwesel, the meandering river Rhine way down below; and if they are very lucky they can spot the "Goethe." It is the last paddle wheel steamer still in operation in the region.

The Rheinsteig hiking trail, which runs alongside the right bank of the Rhine, covers a total distance of 320 km and offers diverse spectacular views. Between Bonn and Wiesbaden it is usually very narrow and leads past castles and palaces, historic villages and lovely vineyards, going uphill and downhill. It is marked throughout.

The excellent transportation infrastructure allows hikers to find a trailhead for each portion of the trail, so that everyone can at least enjoy a section of the popular hike. In addition to the enjoyment of pristine nature, culinary delights abound on the trail that won the remote trail category award "Germany's most beautiful hiking trail 2006."

View from the Rheinsteig hiking trail

View of St. Goar and Rheinfels Castle

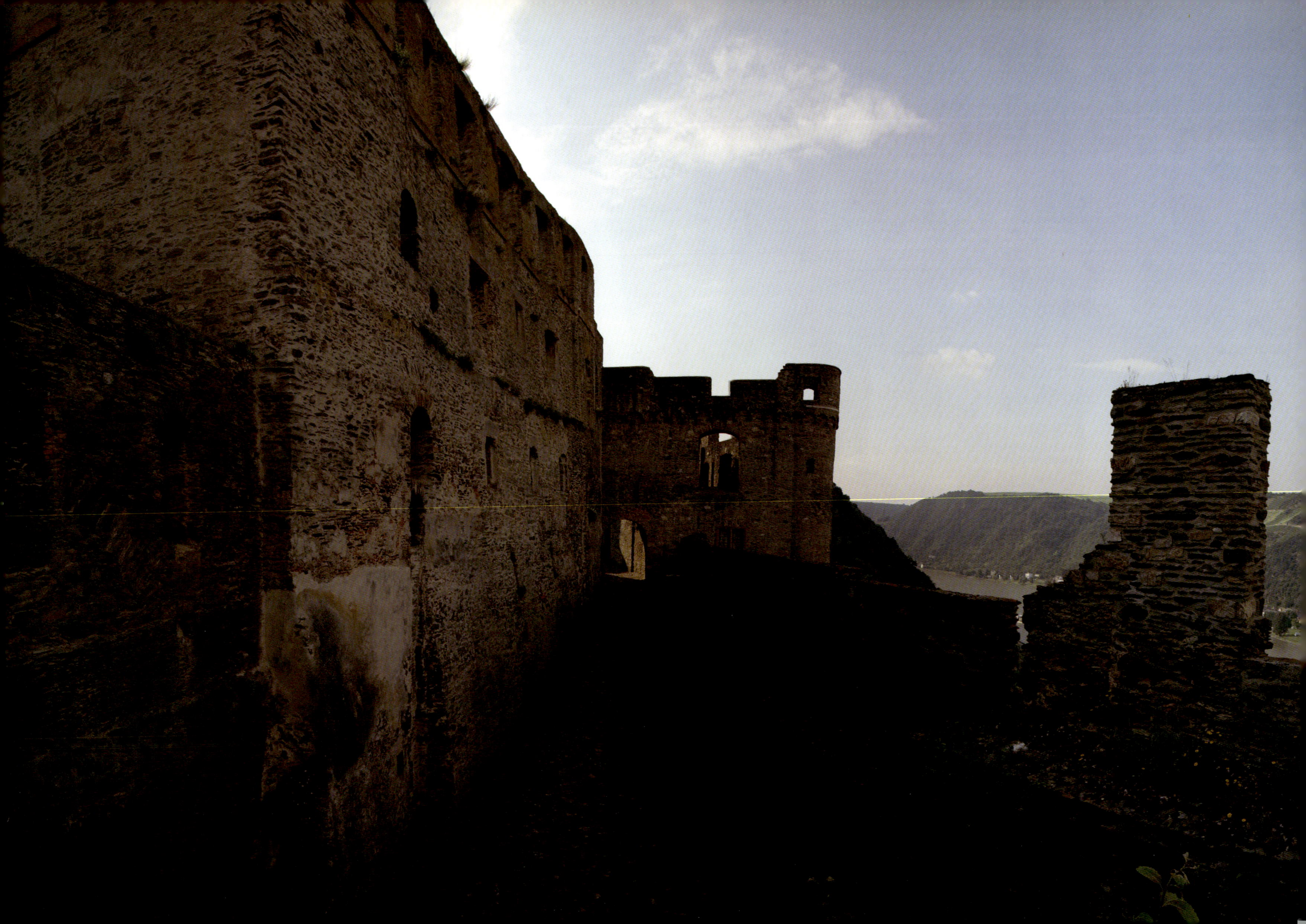

ST. GOAR

Rheinfels Castle

Imposing Rheinfels Castle ruins tower over St. Goar. As a result of numerous expansions it eventually became the largest fortification on the Rhine and was considered tough to conquer. However, the French revolutionary troops blew up the property at the end of the 18th century. A hotel has been located inside the rebuilt part of the castle since 1973. The Rheinfels Path introduces visitors to the history and the magnificent nature that surrounds the gigantic castle lands.

St. Goar was named for Saint Goar who erected a small church and hospital in the new settlement in the 6th century.

St. Goar, which was under the jurisdiction of the Counts of Katzenelnbogen through 1479 and part of the Landgraviate of Hesse through 1794, is now a tourist magnet offering a variety of sights. In the historic city centre, visitors can admire the Saint Goar Church with its ostentatious 11th century Roman crypt, the new gothic Catholic church and the German Doll and Bear Museum as well as the Rhine pilots' museum.

Rheinfells Castle

360° Panorama: Rheinfels Castle above St. Goar 10

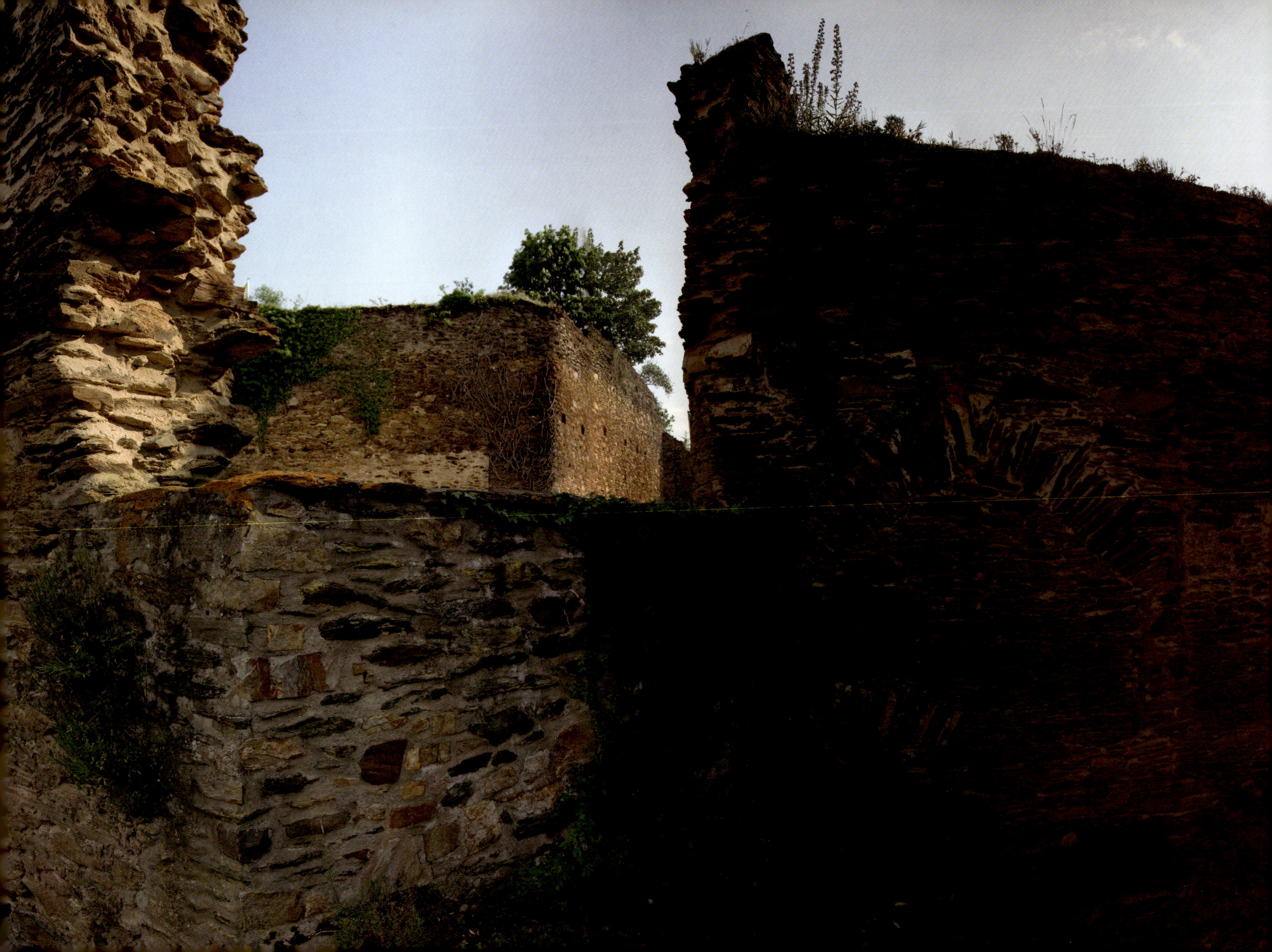

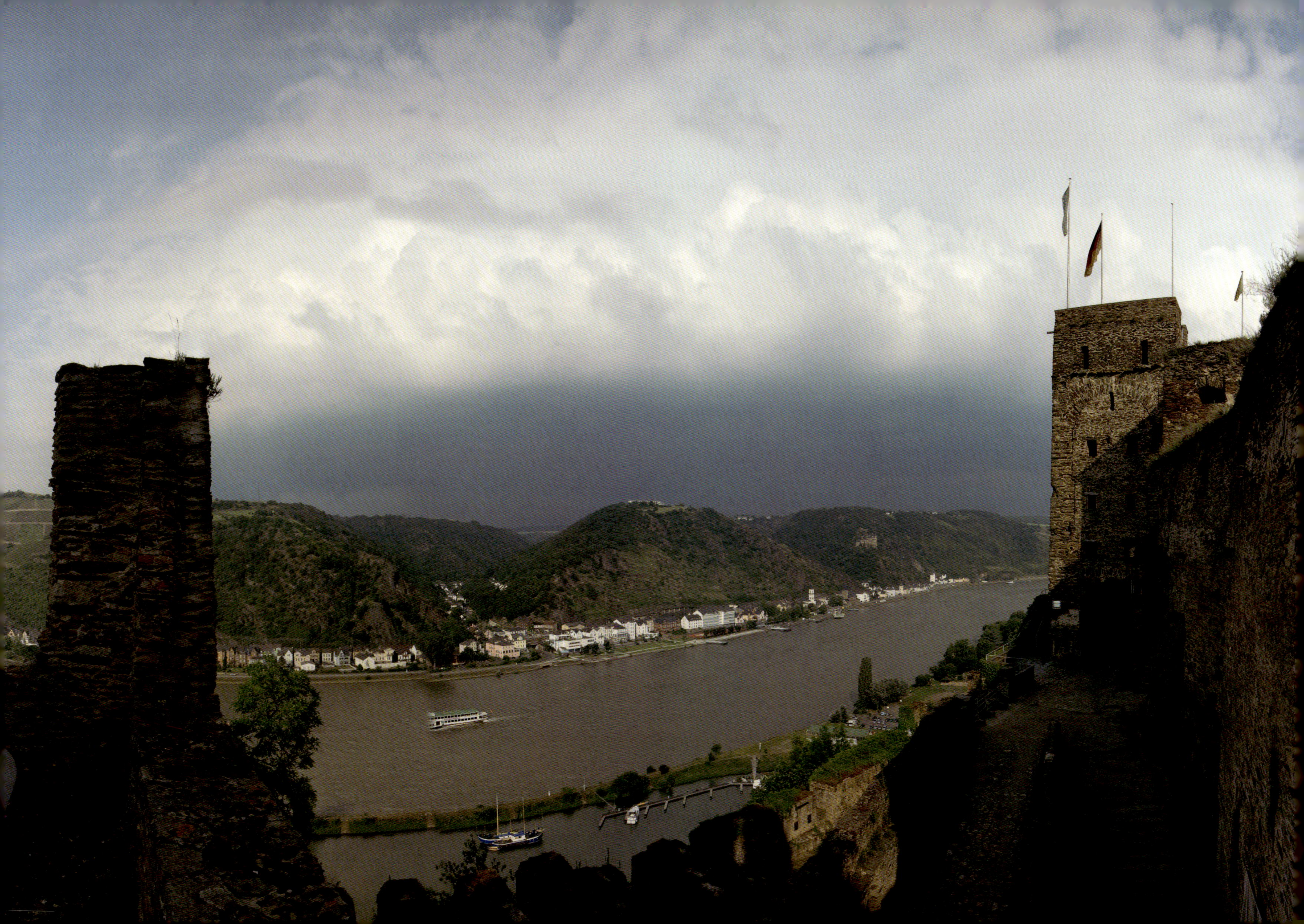

Across the river from St. Goar is St. Goarshausen with its romantic Old Town, two historic town towers and remnants of the town wall. The two towns ensured that Hesse's counts received substantial customs fees. Castles Katz and Maus are perched high above St. Goarshausen. Count William II of Katzenelnbogen started the construction of Katzenelnbogen Castle, nicknamed "Katz" ("Cat"), in circa 1360. As a counter pole to the powerful position of the "Cat" Peterseck was erected from 1362–1388 and nicknamed "Maus" ("Mouse").

The Sculpture Park, an open air art museum, is located between Urbar and Oberwesel. Impressive landscapes and contemporary art are presented in a very harmonious way at this park.

The enchanting small town of Ehrenthal near St. Goarshausen offers a special attraction: A church and a restaurant can be found under one roof. The premises originally housed a monastery. The church, which dates back to this time, was built in honour of Saint Sebastian, whose martyr sacrifice is depicted in a relief behind the altar. The story claiming that the faithful visited the pub while attending services has been labeled pure fiction.

The island Ehrenthaler Werth is offshore from the village in the Rhine.

St. Goarshausen and "Katz" Castle

Fireworks illuminate St. Goar and St. Goarshausen

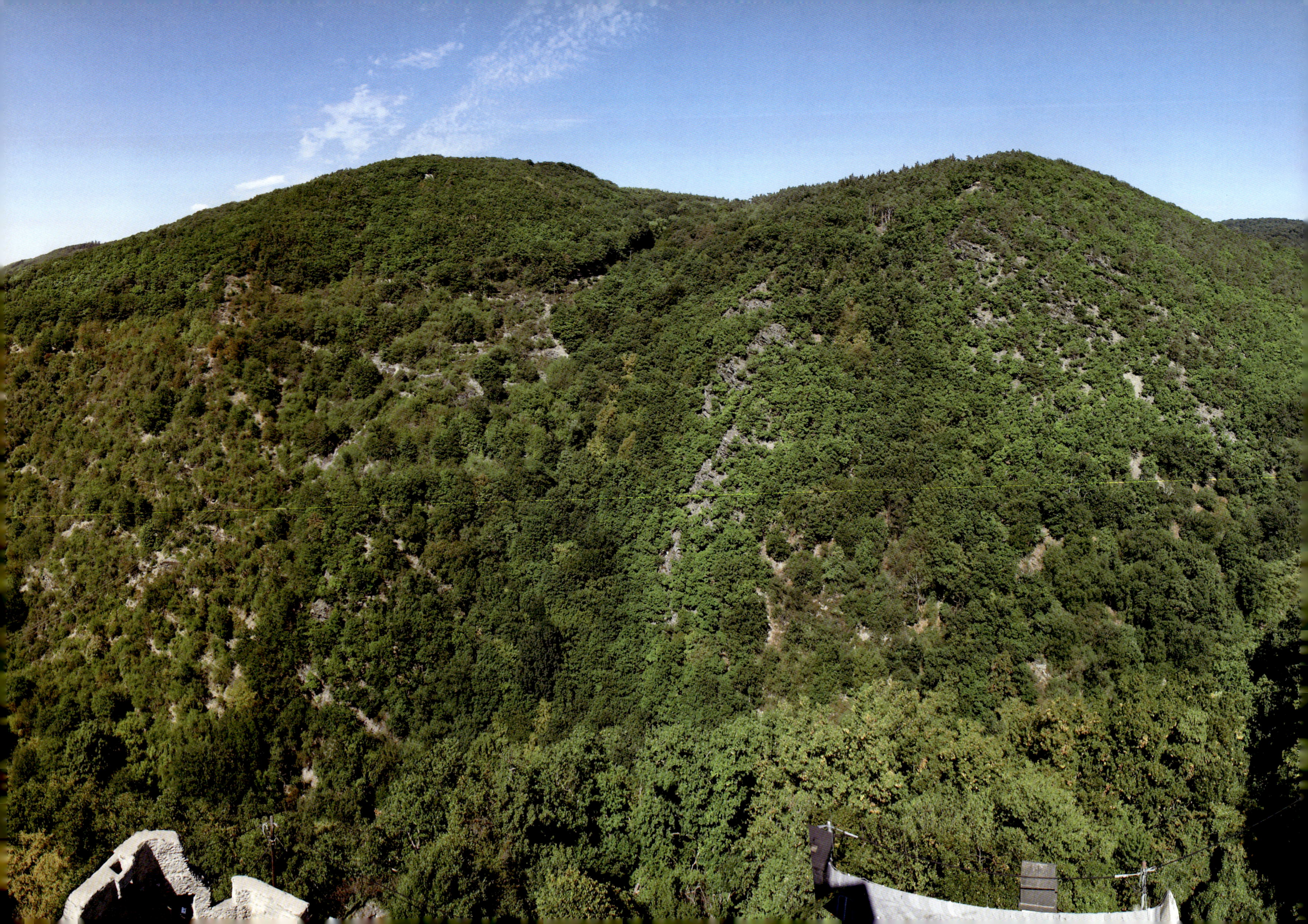

KAMP-BORNHOFEN

"The Hostile Brothers"

Kamp-Bornhofen is a pilgrimage destination with Celtic roots. Two fabled castles tower over the town. Locals call them "The Hostile Brothers". Sterrenberg, the northernmost of the two emerged as early as 1034 and is the oldest castle on the Rhine still standing.

Liebenstein Castle was not built until 1284–90. Two massive protection walls separate castles Sterrenberg and Liebenstein, which is only 200 m to the south. It was once given the nickname "wall of dispute".

The Franciscan monastery of Bornhofen, which dates back to 1224, is a destination for pilgrims from around the globe. Since mediaeval times it has been a venue on the Rhine for unique ship processions, which do not take place at any other pilgrimage site in Germany.

The town of Kamp-Bornhofen made a name for itself as a rafter stronghold. Rafts ceased travelling the Rhine in 1968. The history of raft wood transportation can be experienced in the interesting Rafter and Mariner Museum in Kamp-Bornhofen.

Kamp Bornhofen and "The Hostile Brothers"

360° Panorama: Kamp-Bornhofen – "The Hostile Brothers" **11**

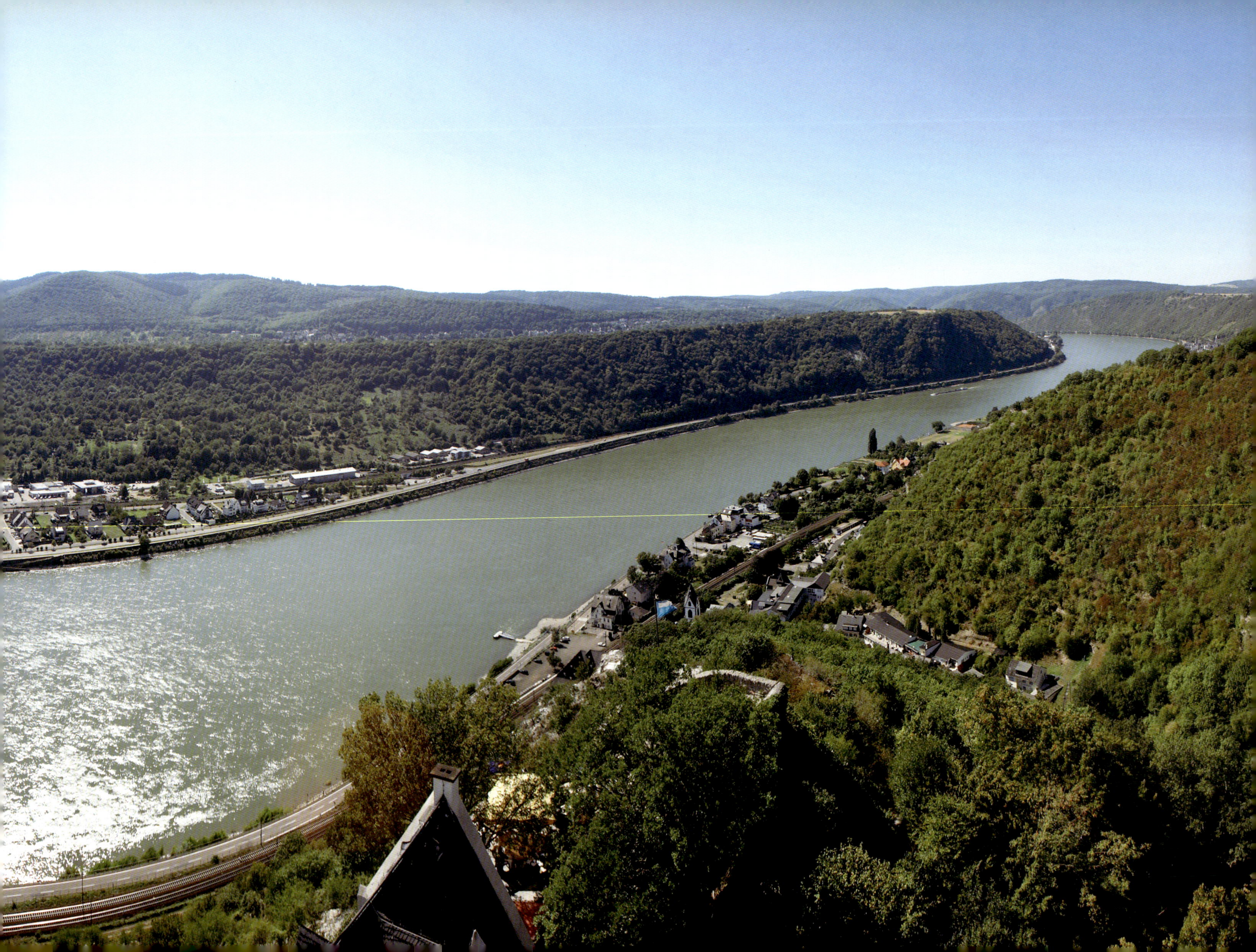

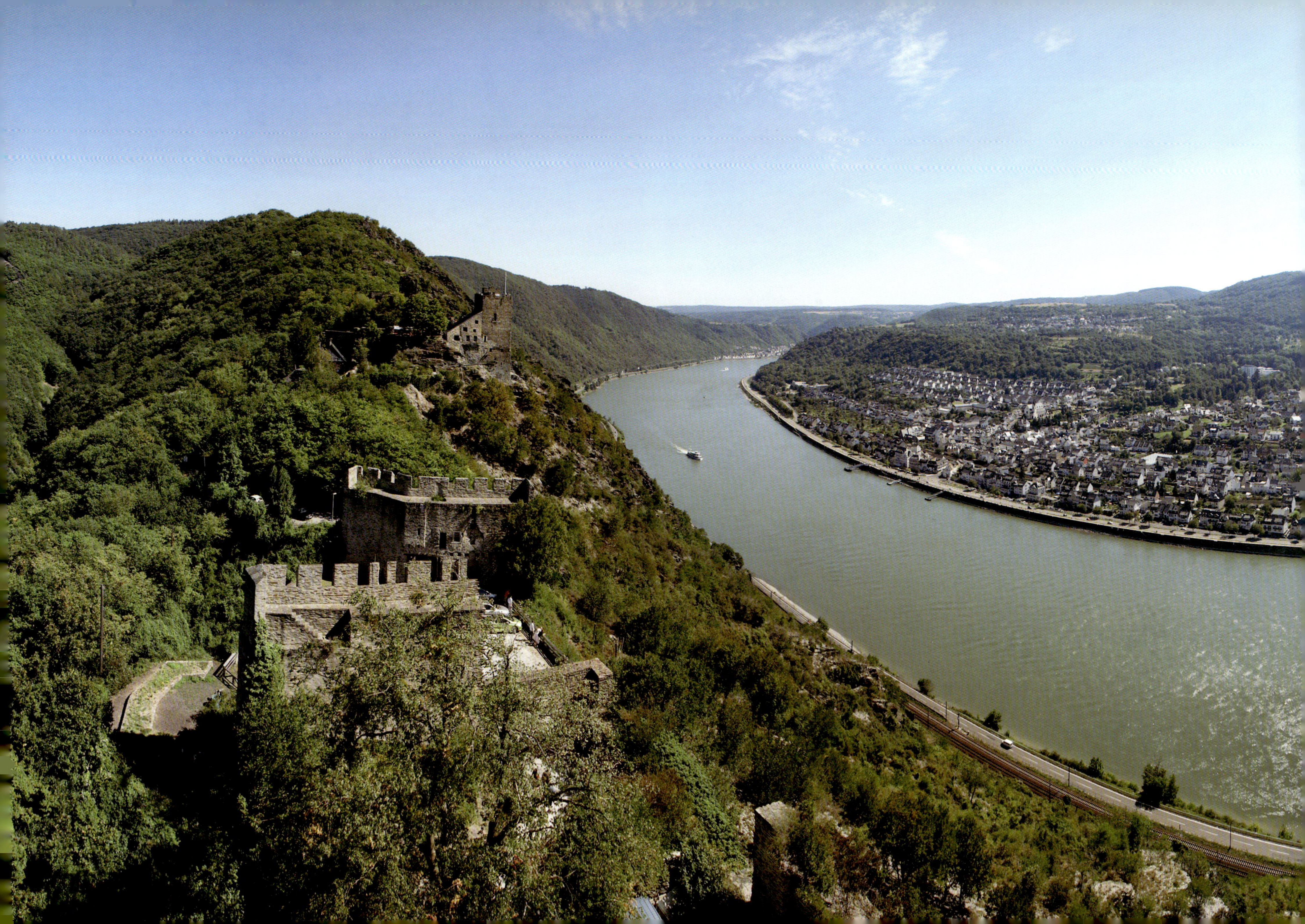

Kamp-Bornhofen

Franciscan Pilgrimage Monastery Bornhofen

Kestert, north of Ehrenthal, made its first public records appearance in 1110 as a Roman settlement called "Kestene" and has all the looks of a Rhine romanticism village. It is a popular destination and an ideal vantage point for visits to the many cultural and geographic sights of the Rhine Valley, the Moselle and the Lahn.

From the 385 m elevation of the Hindenburghöhe lookout, one can indulge in fascinating panoramic views across the Rhine and of the surrounding vineyards. In addition to numerous enthralling half-timbered houses, the romantic town offers sights such as the Saint George's Church, built from 1778 to 1779. Spring is a particularly enchanting time to come here, as the innumerable fruit trees are in full bloom.

Bad Salzig on the opposite side of the Rhine is known for its mineral spa and acquired the right to bear the name "Bad Salzig" in 1925. Springs containing sodium sulphate erupted here in 1902 and 1905 from a depth of 446 m. Nestled into the valley of creek Salzborn, the village offers fascinating views across the Rhine and of Sterrenberg and Liebenstein castles. Thanks to its moderate climate, the picturesque town is also a first rate fruit cultivation area.

The Rhine near Kestert

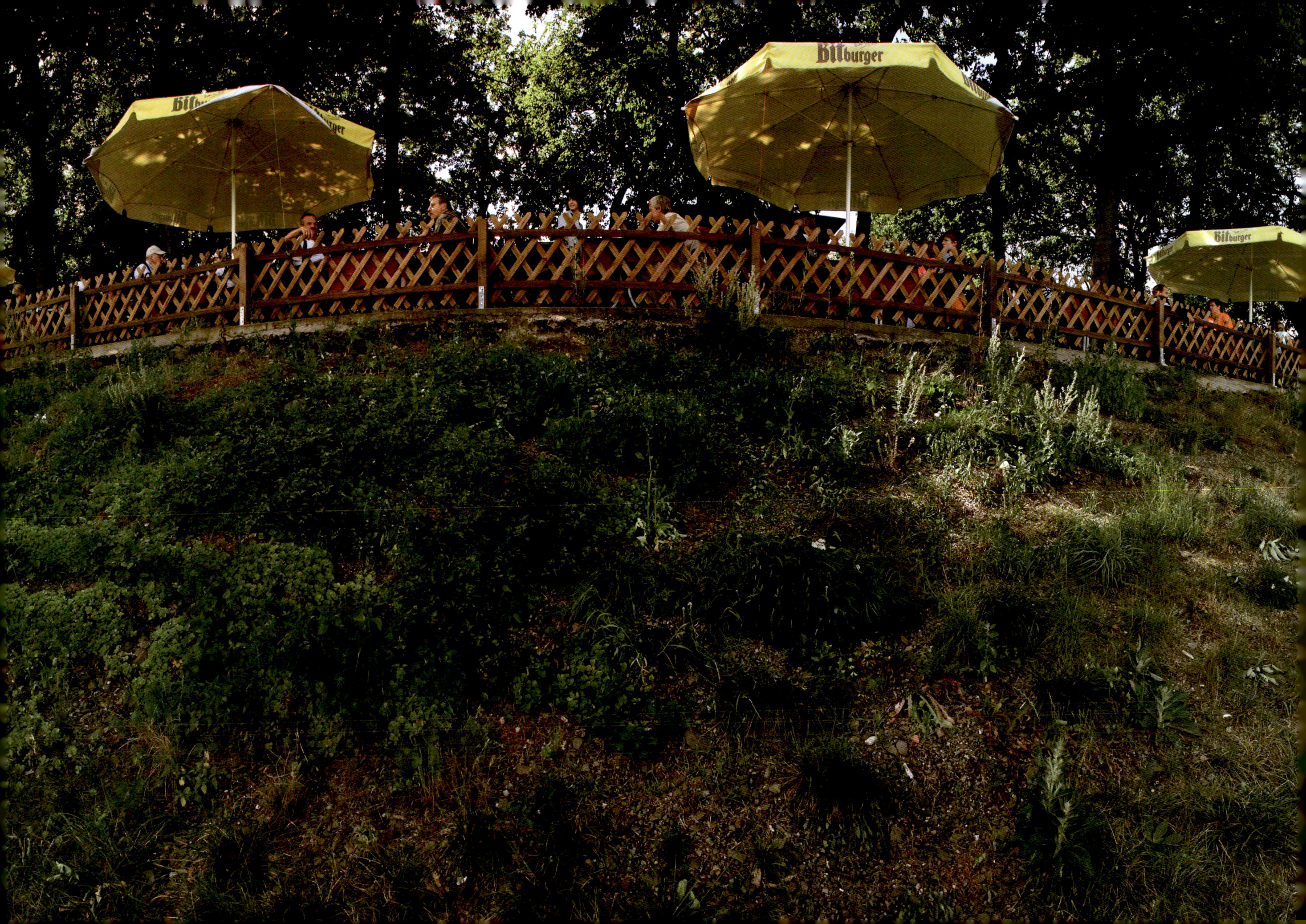
Bitburger

BOPPARD

Gedeonseck

Boppard is located on the western bank of the upper Middle Rhine, the section of the Rhine included in the list of world heritage sites in 2002. The name Boppard can be traced back to the pre-Christian Celtic settlement "Bodobrica". The Romans built a castle here in the first centuries after the birth of Christ. The stone fortress with 28 semi-circular towers is one of the best preserved Roman fortresses in Northern Europe. Boppard's first early Christian church was built in its former thermal bath. Today, the pulpit and baptismal font lie under the stone floor of the late Roman Saint Severus Church from the 12th century. Parts of the mediaeval city wall remain intact, including the gorgeous Bingen Gate. The 14th century electoral castle, which houses the city museum, is on the banks of the Rhine. Other sights worth seeing include the 15th century Knight Schwalbach House, the Carmelite Church from the 14th and 15th centuries and the former Marienberg monastery, founded in 1120.

With the "Bopparder Hamm" the city has the largest contiguous appellation on the Middle Rhine. The famous Gedeonseck outlook towers above Boppard. The Rhine forms a large loop at Boppard, within which lie the towns of Osterspai and Filsen amidst a fruit-growing area. Liebeneck Castle, which rises above the municipality of Osterspai, was originally built in 1590 by the gentlemen of Liebenstein and was restored between 1977 and 1978. The famous Vierseenblicklift (a chair lift with a view to the so-called "four lakes" of the Rhine) takes visitors from Boppard to the 230 m high Hirschkopf.

Four lakes lookout point

360° Panorama: Boppard – Gedeonseck **12**

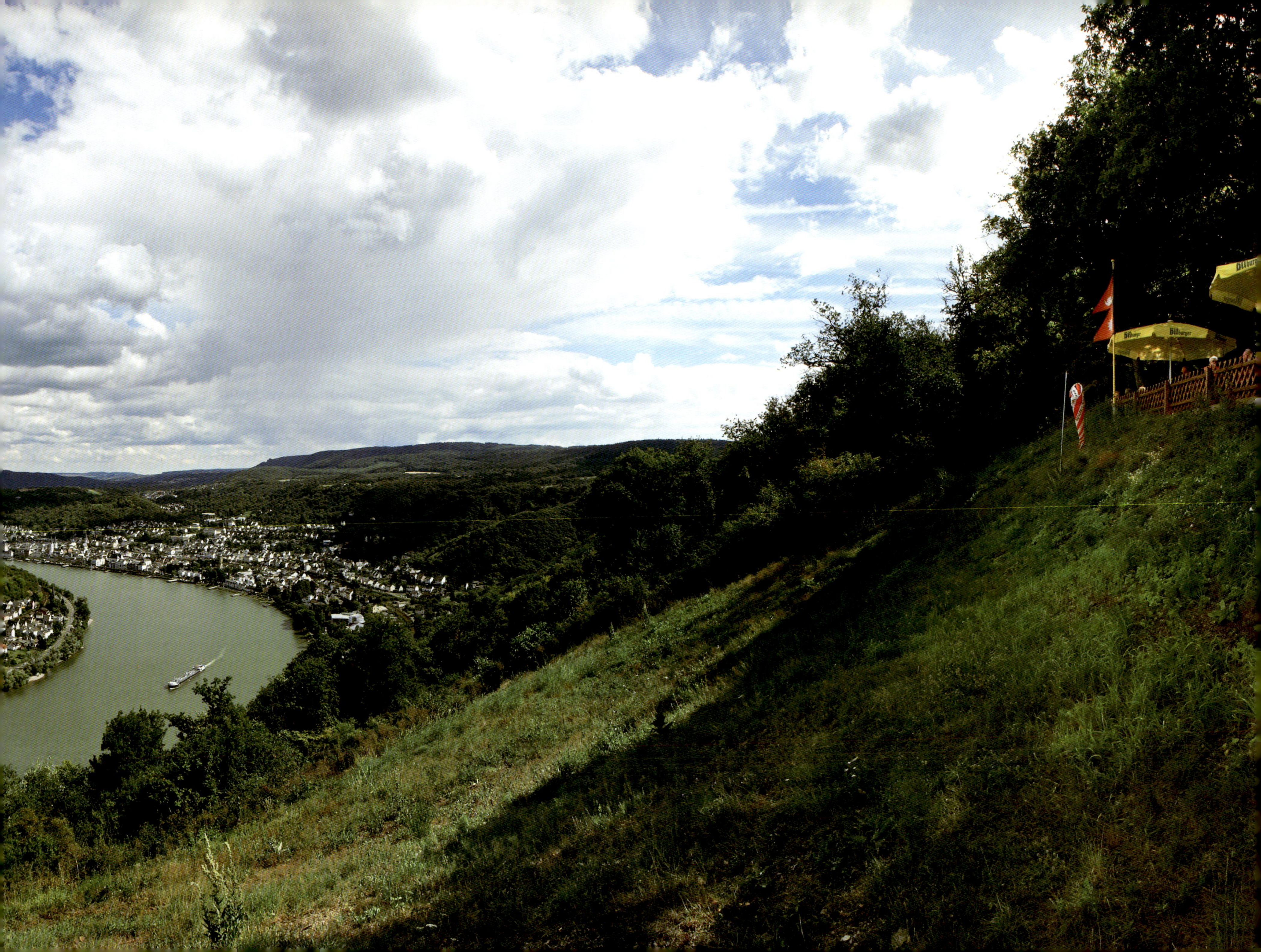
Bitburger
Bitburger

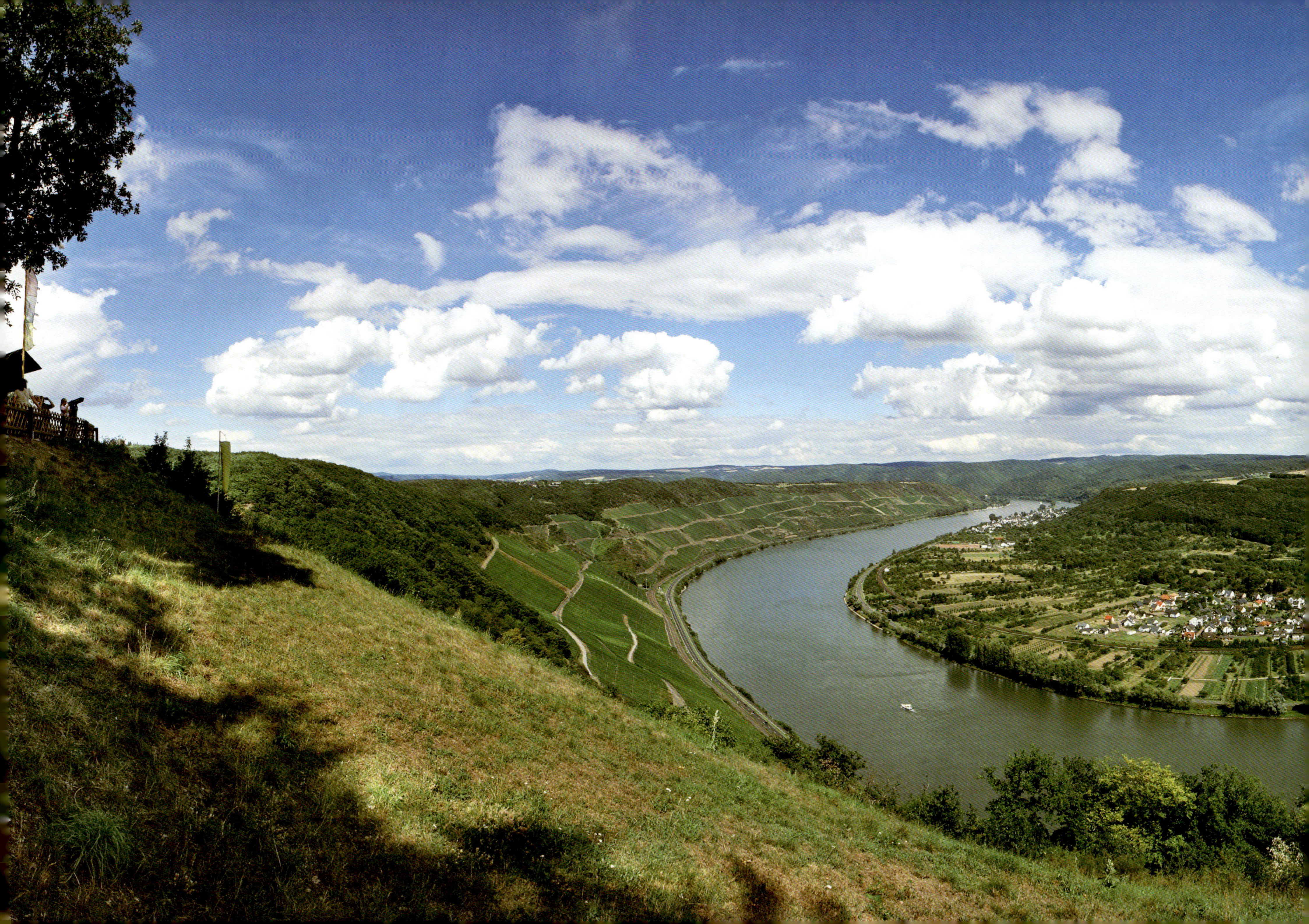

The picturesque wine-growing town of Hirzenach, which is part of the municipality of Boppard, is located on the opposite bank of the Rhine. The town is largely dominated by the buildings of a former former abbey of the Order of Saint Benedict.

Spay, located north of Boppard, was first mentioned in documents in 816. The town's attractions include half-timbered houses from the 17th and 18th centuries, Peter's Chapel which was built in 1300, and Saint Lambertus parish church from 1899.

The town of Brey, located north of Spay, dates back to Roman times. The 4.5 metre deep Roman aqueduct, which was broken through shale is evidence of this. The town, which is over 1,100 years old, boasts many impressive half-timbered structures including the Town Hall from 1514, the parish churches Saint Dionysius and Saint Theresia and the Scharfenturm from the 13th or 14th century.

Rhens is especially known for its mineral spring, from which water has been bottled for more than 150 years. The present-day "Königsstuhl von Rhens" (King's Chair of Rhens) on the bank of the Rhine is a huge throne from 1842. The original was a wooden structure that was built before 1398 and was destroyed in 1795.

The history of the city of Lahnstein dates back to the 3rd century. Lahnstein was heavily fortified in the 14th century and the city wall comprised Martinsburg Castle, which was built in 1298. The remains of the city fortification, such as the Hexenturn (Witches' Tower) from 1324, have been preserved to this day.

Sights worth seeing in the Oberlahnstein quarter include the Salhof, a half-timbered structure from the 15th century that was first mentioned in public records in 977. Today, the Salhof houses the town archives. Visitors will also enjoy the impressive parish church Saint Martin with towers from 1190 and the Johanniskloster, a monastery from 1130, the "Wirtshaus an der Lahn" (Inn on the Lahn) which was built in 1697, and the Allerheiligenkapelle, a chapel from the end of the 19th century.

Located at the mouth of the Lahn in the Rhine, the picturesque Lahneck Castle offers a typical eye-catching glimpse of Rhine romanticism. It was built from 1240–45, destroyed in 1688 and its ruins inspired Goethe's poem "Geistesgruß" in 1744.

Reconstruction work on Lahneck Castle began in 1852. It is part of the Upper Middle Rhine Valley UNESCO World Heritage Site.

Lahneck Castle above Oberlahnstein

The small town of Braubach is located on the eastern bank of the Rhine across from Spay. The Marksburg, which sits on top of a rock cone just above the town, is the only mountain castle on the Middle Rhine that was never destroyed. Its state of preservation is exceptional and it boasts the original 12th century structural substance, which was expanded in Gothic style in the 14th century. It houses a castle museum that is worth visiting.

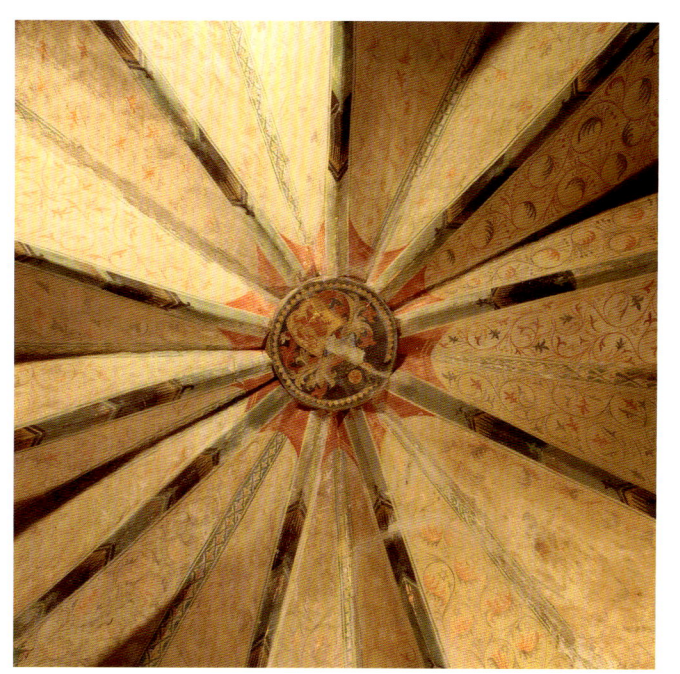

Impressions of the Marksburg

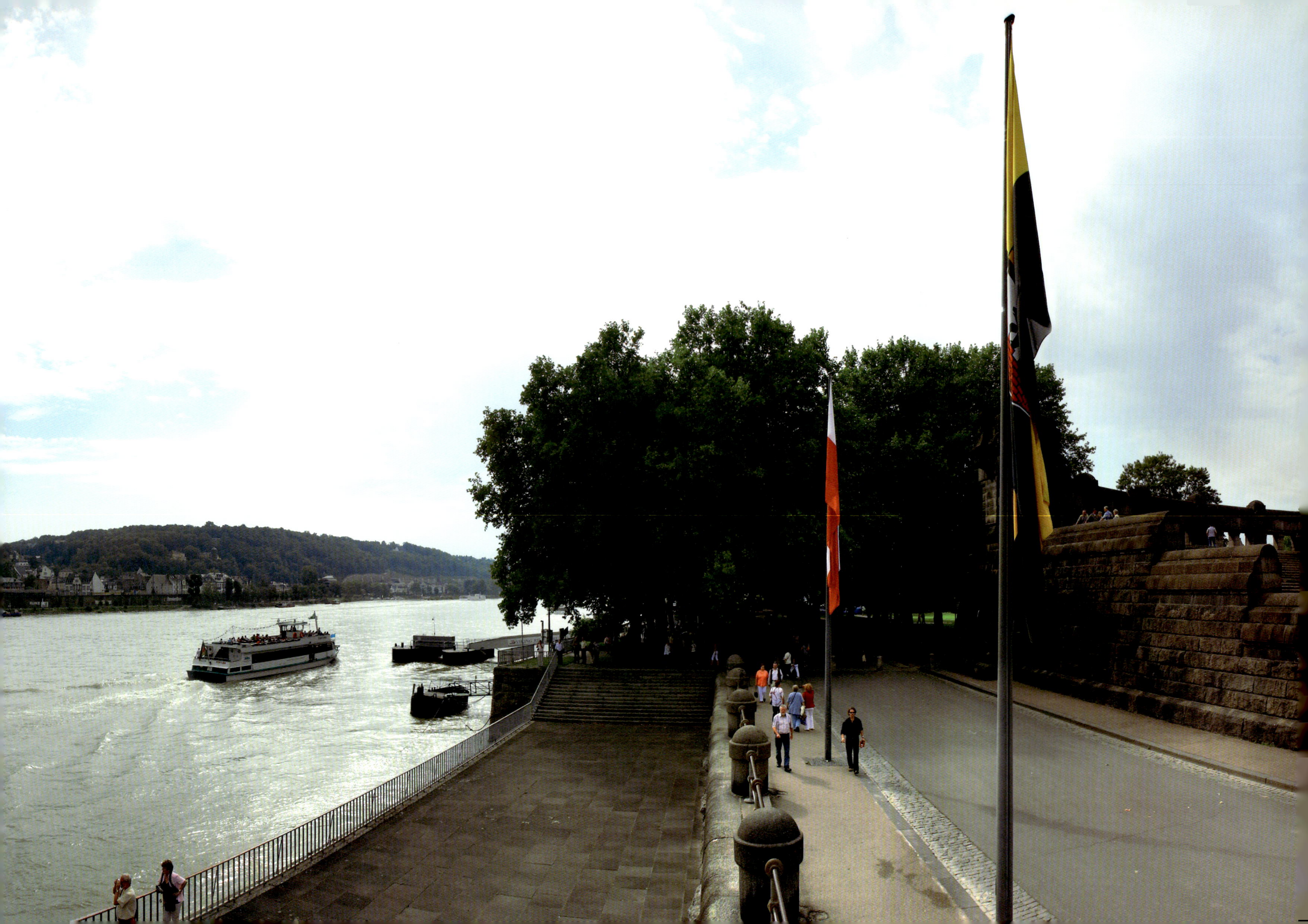

KOBLENZ

Deutsches Eck

Koblenz, one of the oldest and most beautiful cities in Germany, lies right at the Rhine/Moselle estuary. The first settlements date back to the Middle Stone Age. The archaeological excavation of an ancient palisade from 1000 BC at Festung Ehrenbreitstein proved that a fortress once stood here around 250 years before the founding of Rome.

On a hook right where the Mosel meets the Rhine, the Teutonic Order built the so-called Deutschherrenhaus (House of the Teutonic Knights) in the 13th century. This site was quickly named "Deutsches Eck". Today, the Deutsche Eck with its 1891 equestrian statue of Emperor Wilhelm I is a world-famous tourist attraction. The 37 m high monument depicts the emperor sitting on a horse accompanied by the goddess of victory, and commemorates German Unification, which was achieved from 1864–1871. A short distance away, Balduinbrücke (Baldwin's Bridge) spans the Mosel. The stone arch bridge dates back to the 14th century and is the oldest preserved bridge in Koblenz.

All over the city area are remains of the casemates and ramparts. The remains of the walls of Feste Kaiser Alexander from 1817–1822 and the Löwentor are located in the Karthause quarter. Parts of the building substance of other fortification of Emperor Franz, Fort Asterstein and the Pfaffendorf Hill have been preserved. Fort Großfürst Konstantin, a former monastery that was first mentioned in public records in 1153, now houses the Rhenish Carnival Museum.

Among the most beautiful architectural landmarks are the 13th century Alte Burg (Old Castle), the 18th century Electorate Castle, the stately Prussian government building erected from 1902–06, the Deutschherrenhaus dating back to 1214 with the Ludwig Museum and the birth house of the mother of Ludwig van Beethoven in the Ehrenbreitstein quarter.

The oldest church in Koblenz is the Basilica Saint Kastor, whose roots reach back to 817. Visitors can marvel at the birth house of Prince Metternich in the Münzplatz, and the History Column in the Görresplatz.

"Rhine in flames" over Ehrenbreitstein

360° Panorama: Koblenz – Deutsches Eck **13**

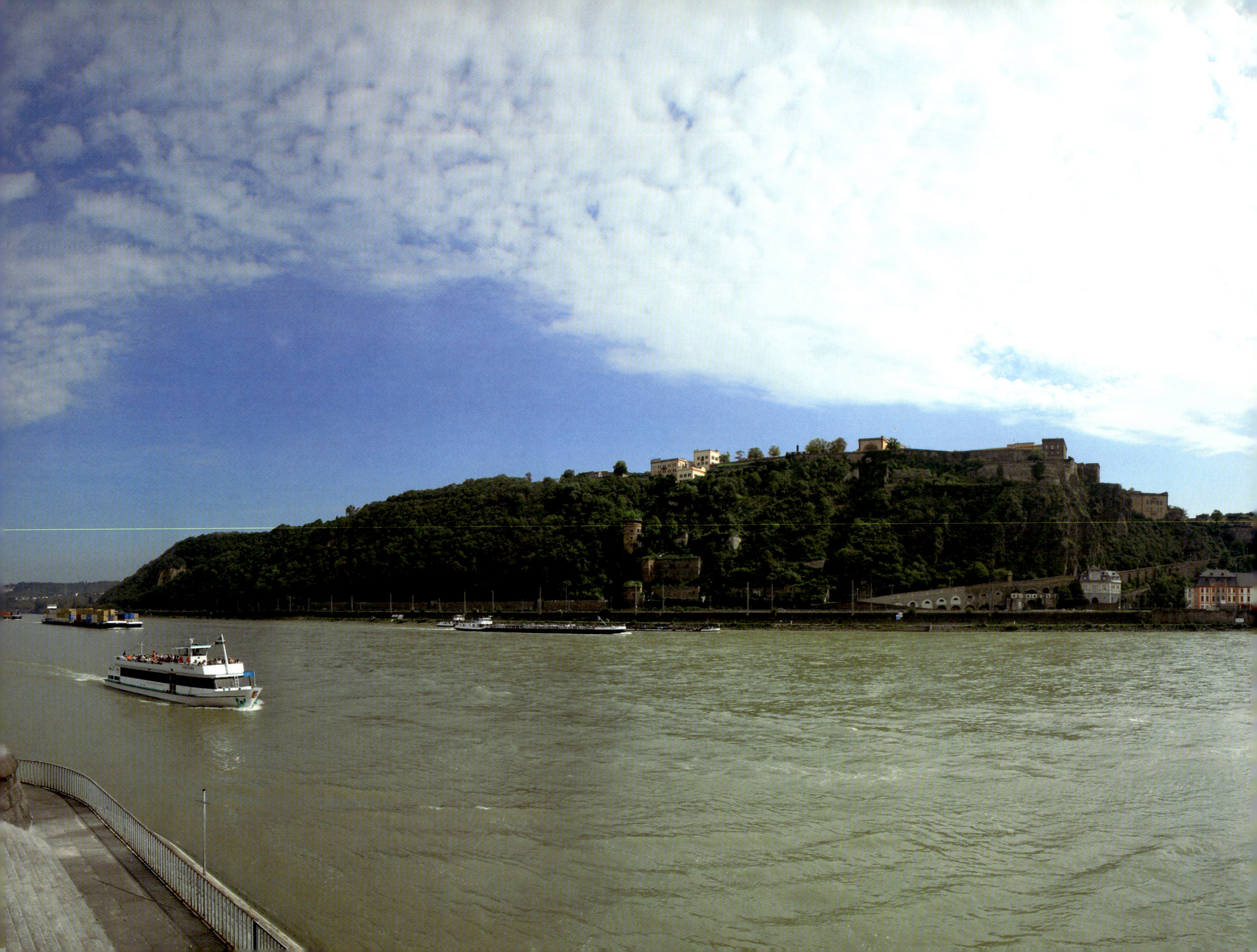

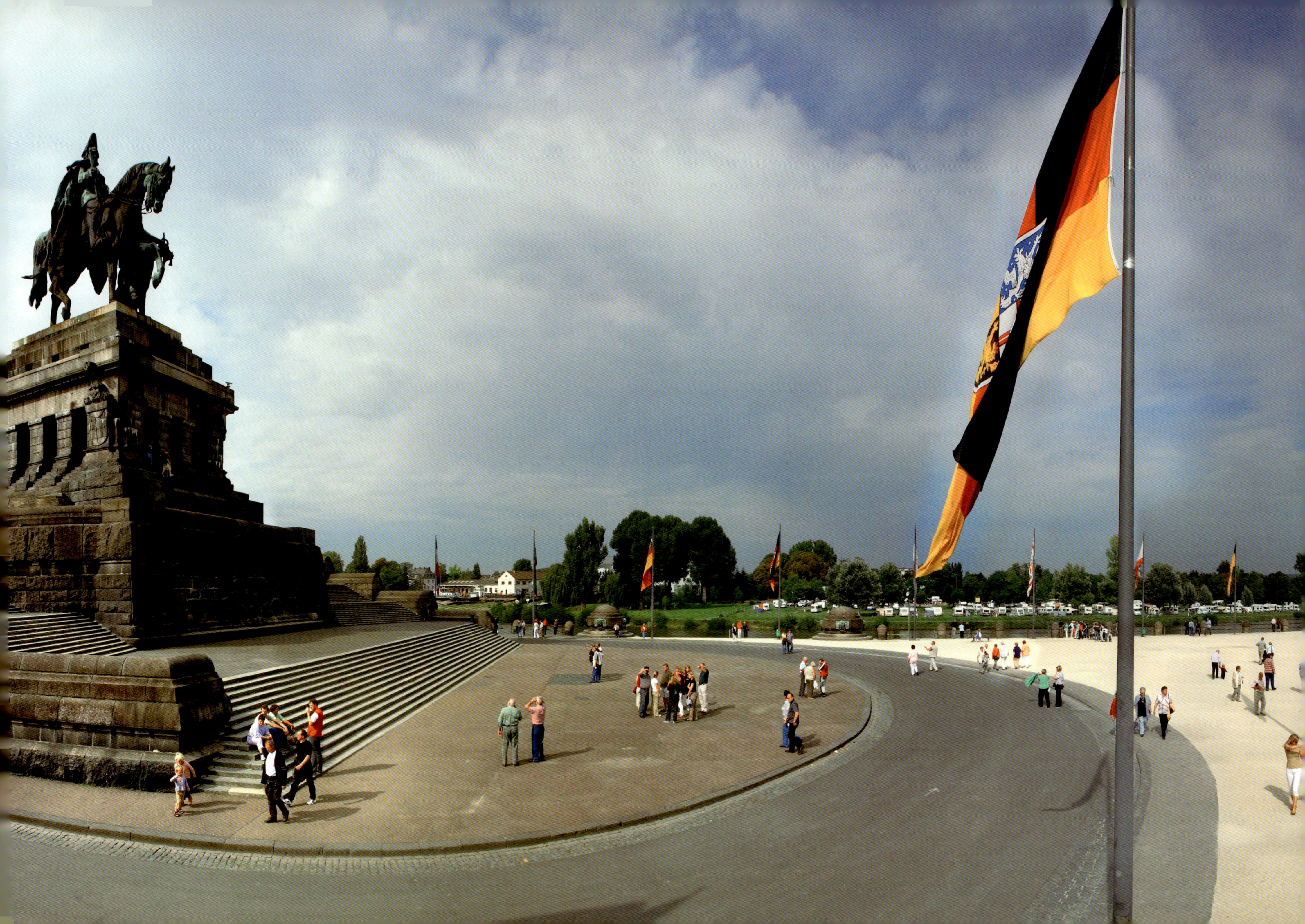

The "Schängelbrunnen" (scallywag fountain) in town hall square was built in 1940. It is a monument to the rascals born here and is one of the town's landmarks.

Modern urban life unfolds here between historical buildings. Koblenz offers a wide range of stages and museums, and is known for its alternative music scene. The Koblenz carnival, whose roots reach back to the 13th century, is an annual cultural highlight.

Koblenz-Oberwerth lies on a former Rhine island. An aristocratic Benedictine convent was built here in 1142 and was not dissolved until 1802 in the course of secularisation.

Oberwerth is connected to the traffic system via the Horchheim railway bridge and the Südbrücke (Southern Bridge). The 236 m long Südbrücke was built from 1969 to 1975 and is one of the most important traffic routes crossing the Rhine.

In 1948 Koblenz was the venue for a multiple-day conference of West German minister presidents, in which the groundwork for the founding of West Germany and its Basic Law were negotiated. A monument to this memorable event was erected in 1978 on the imposing Rittersturz lookout point.

The "Schängelbrunnen"

View of the Alte Burg from Balduinbrücke

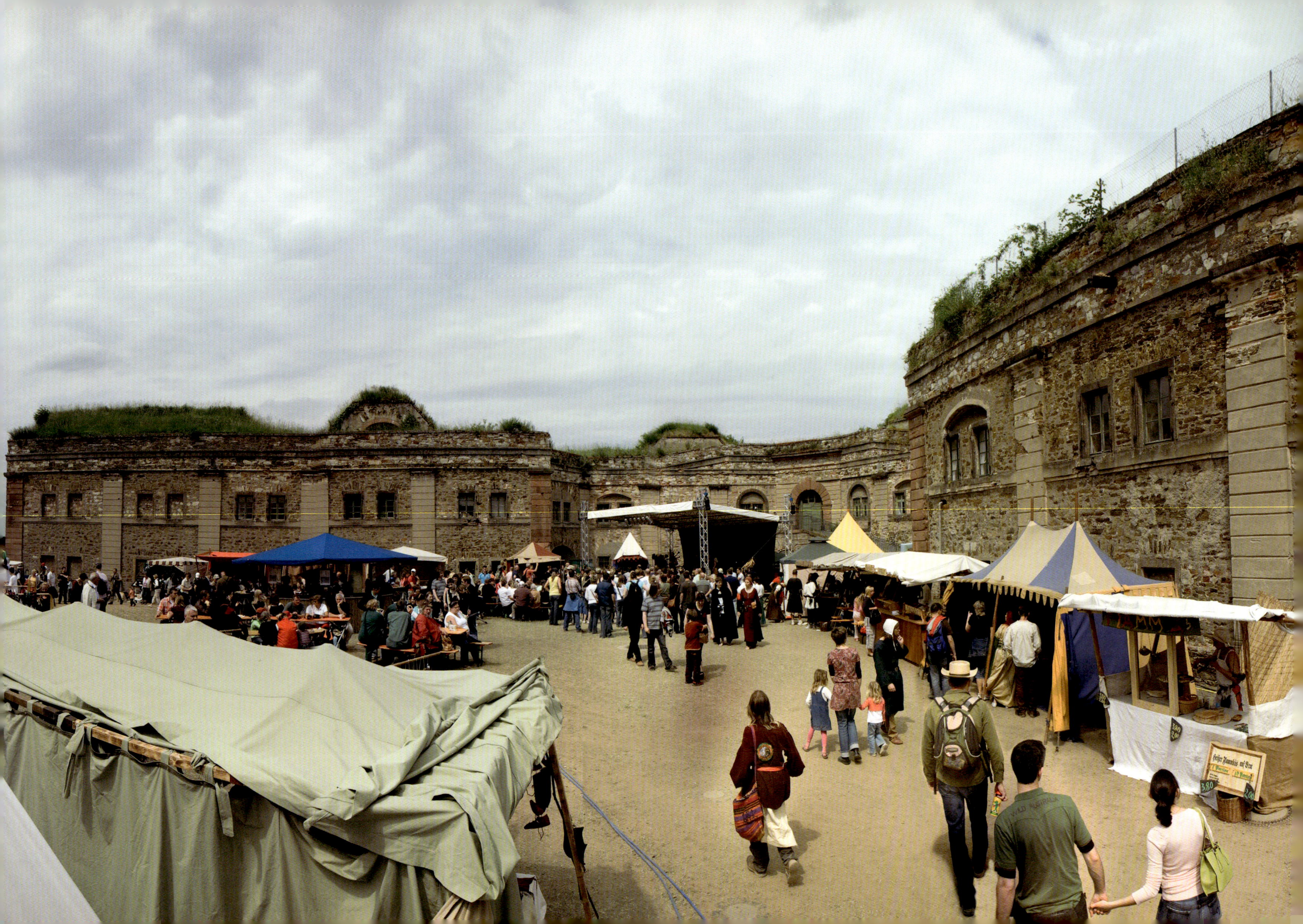

Festung Ehrenbreitstein

A fortress on the mountain Ehrenbreitstein opposite to Koblenz was first mentioned in public records in 1000. Monumental bastions of Electoral Trier and Prussian dominance emerged here between the 16th and 19th centuries that bore witness to the battle of the Rhine. For a long time, the fortress was considered impregnable. The largest cannon, the Greif Cannon, weighs an impressive nine tonnes and is 4.5 m long. Today, life in this once defensive site is peaceful: It houses the Koblenz Landesmuseum.

The small town of Vallendar, a well known Kneipp and climatic spa, is located north of Ehrenbreitstein. This historical town was first mentioned in public records in the 9th century and boasts beautiful half-timbered buildings from the 17th century. The parish church Saint Marzellinus and Saint Peter from the 19th century, the Wiltberger Hof from 1695–98, the Marienburg Chapel, the Emperor Frederick look-out tower at the nearby Mallendarer Berg are all worth visiting as well. Vallendar is characterised by the Schönstatt pilgrimage monastery. The first Augustine monastery emerged in the Schönstatt district in 1143. Since 1901 numerous religious educational buildings of the Catholic Pallottines have emerged on the site, which draws countless pilgrims from all over the world.

In front of Vallendar lies the island of Niederwerth with the municipality of the same name. It is Germany's only independent island municipality. A monastery complex was located on the southern shore from the 15th to the 19th centuries; the former monastery church, consecrated in 1474, has been preserved as the Saint Georg Church.

The fortress Festung Ehrenbreitstein

360°-Panoramafoto: Koblenz – Festung Ehrenbreitstein **14**

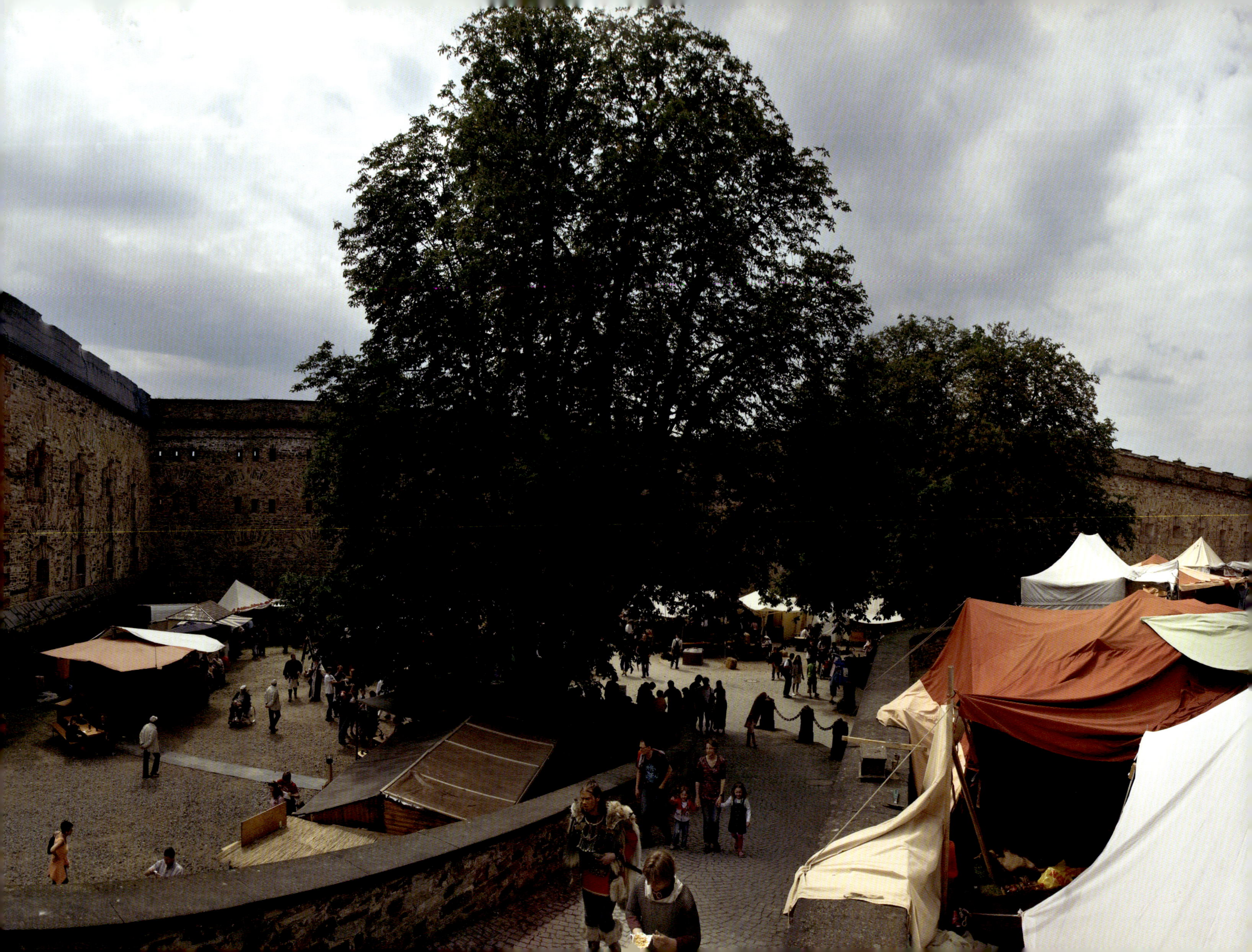

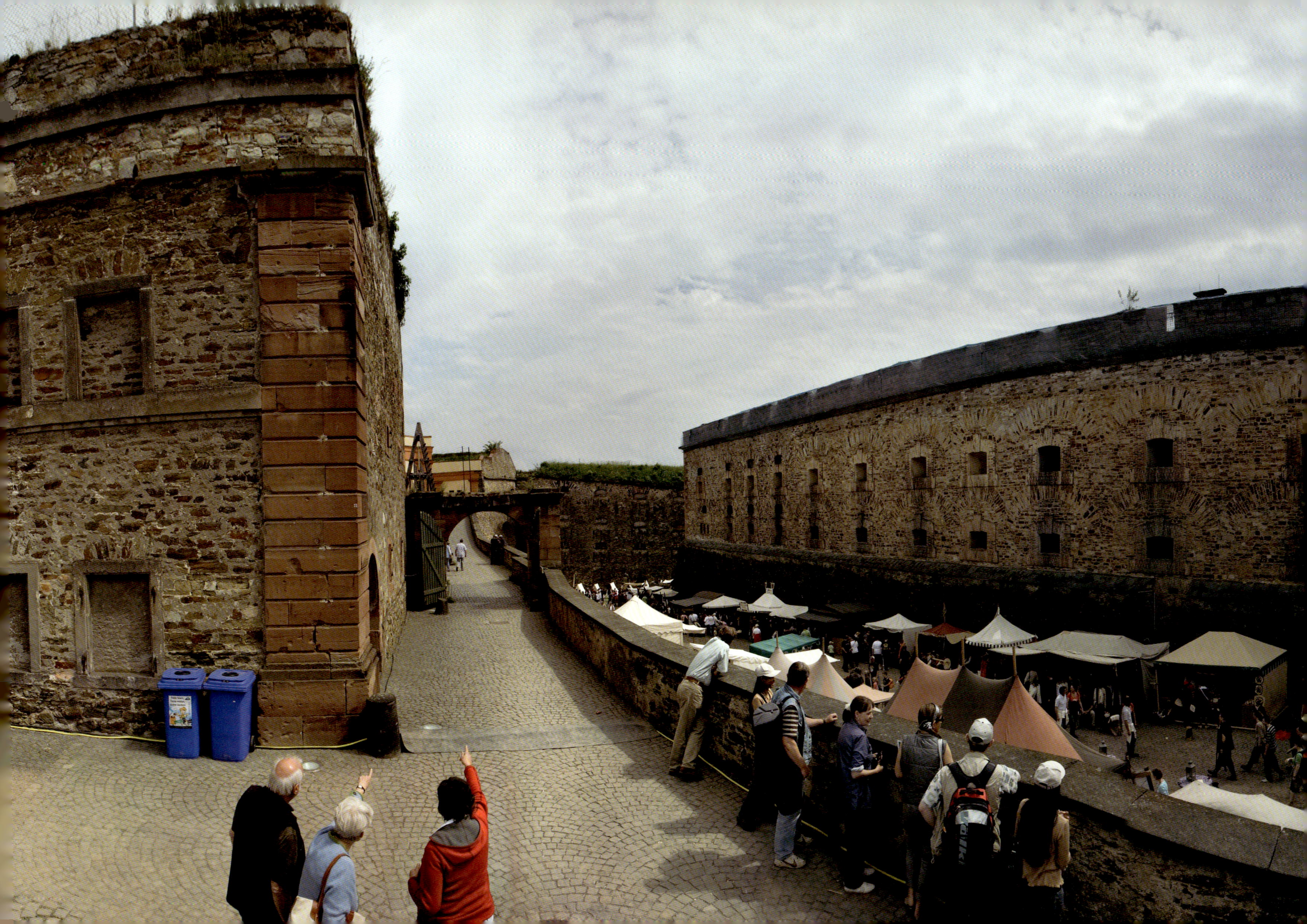

The settlement history of the historic Rhine town of Bendorf, located north of Vallendar on the German Limes Route, dates back to before the birth of Christ. An earthen castle and iron smelteries attest to the Roman times that followed. The town was first mentioned in documents in 948. The abbey was founded in 1201 in the present-day Sayn district.

Characterised by mining and metallurgy, the city today is a lively and romantic shopping and tourist destination. The ensemble of the Protestant parish church and the St. Medardus Catholic parish church is impressive. The Haus Remy from 1747, in which Goethe once stopped by for a bite to eat, and a worker's house from the 19th century in Friedensreich Hundertwasser style are also worth seeing. Every year, Bendorf organises the largest Christmas market in the Middle Rhine.

The magnificent Sayn Palace is located in the Sayn district. Built in the 19th century and restored in the 20th century, it now houses the Rhenish Iron Casting Art Museum. Above the palace lie the ruins of Sayn Castle, the former family seat of the counts of Sayn-Wittgenstein from the 12th century. Next to the well preserved donjon, a wildlife park and falconry draw innumerable visitors. In 2007 the former Prussian Sayn Ironworks was nominated for the historical landmark of engineering architecture in Germany award.

Engers, the present-day Neuwied district, is considered the oldest Roman settlement on the right bank of the Rhine. This is where a bridge was presumably built across the Rhine in 55 BC under Julius Caesar. The Romans later built a harbour in Engers as well as a castle, the vestiges of which remain until present day.

Engers Castle, located directly on the Rhine, was built as an electoral hunting lodge and summer residence from 1759 to 1764. The late Baroque castle building now houses the national music foundation Villa Musica and a museum. The old town hall from 1642 and castle tavern from 1621 are located opposite the castle courtyard. Parts of the city fortifications have been preserved, such as the "Graue Turm" (Grey Tower) from the 14th century.

The town of Urmitz is located opposite the island of Urmitzer Werth on the western bank of the Rhine. The town, which was first mentioned in documents in the 8th century, is known for cultivating pumice, but is renowned as being the location of the most important rampart and trench system on the Middle Rhine. Other discoveries allude to a settlement as early as the 3rd or 5th centuries BC. The emblem of the city, which is visible from a long distance, is considerably younger - the Baroque church St. Georg from 1772. An Urmitz railway bridge has connected both banks of the Rhine since 1954. The previous structure from 1916–1918, called the Kronprinz-Wilhelm-Brücke (Crown Prince William Bridge), was blown up around the end of World War II.

Weißenthurm, north of Urmitz, is named after a border tower between the Trier and Cologne electorates from 1370. Today, the White Tower is an important tourist attraction for the city and comprises the "Heimatmuseum". The Rhine island of Weißenthurmer Werth is located upstream from the town.

Neuwied, settled as early as Celtic and Roman times, was appointed a city in 1653 and quickly developed into a centre of tolerance. Its citizens were the first in Germany to enjoy freedom of press, of trade and of religion and exemption from taxation – unfortunately, the latter did not survive to the present day.

A thriving industry evolved early on In Neuwied, the only city on the Rhine to be safeguarded by a flood protection dam. The city boasts a myriad of architectural and cultural attractions. Neuwied Castle is the former residential palace of the counts and princes of Wied. It replaced the 12th century Altwied Castle – now interesting ruins – as the ancestral seat of the counts. Neuwied Castle was built in the 18th century. The complex which is surrounded by a picturesque castle garden, is still the Wied family residence, thus private. The Princess' Palace which was built in 1909 and was once part of the castle Monrepos. now houses the Museum of Ice Age Archaeology.

Visitors to Neuwied are impressed by the plethora of important monastery and church buildings, including a former Rommersdorf Premonstratensian abbey from the 12th century and church Feldkirche. Numerous historical buildings are found in the Old Town: The brewery from 1694, the Old Town Hall from 1740, the "Alte Zollamt" (Old Customs Office) from 1696 and the former Roentgen house of 1776 deserve particular mention. The new bridge Raiffeisenbrücke between Neuwied and Weißenthurm was completed in 1978 and is a symbol of the town. There is also a large marina for boat traffic.

Andernach Rhine promenade

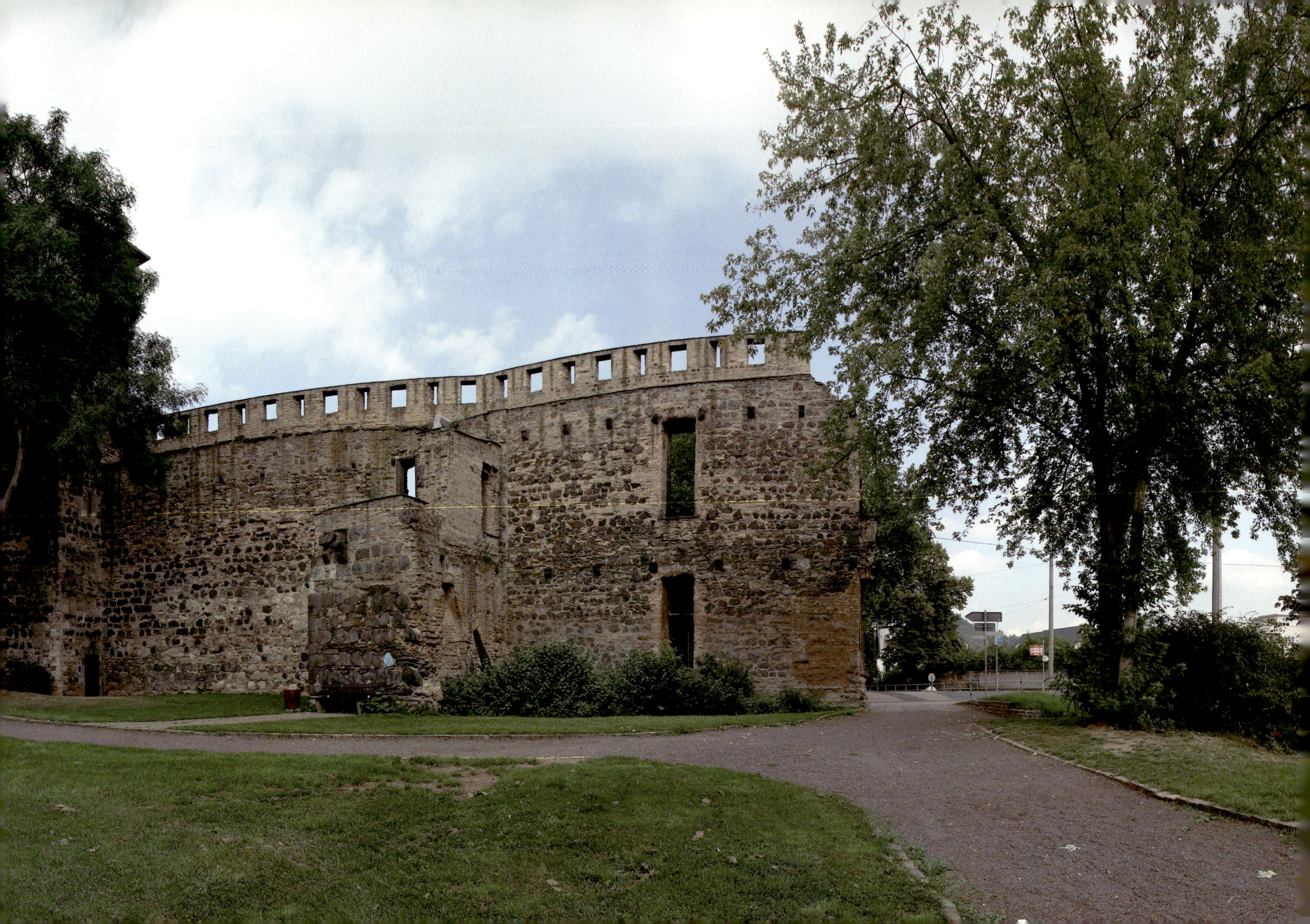

ANDERNACH

City Castle

Andernach which is situated on the western bank of the Rhine, has a settlement history dating back to before the Stone Age and is one of the oldest cities in Germany. Surrounded by a wide moat, the city castle "Stadtburg" was destroyed by French troops in 1698. Parts of the former city fortification are still intact, for example the "Hauptturm" (Main Tower), built in 1370, the "Koblenzer Tor" (Koblenz Gate) from 1450, the "Pulverturm" (Powder Tower) from 1519 and the "Rheintor" (Rhine Gate), which was built in 1200 and restored in 1899.

The 55 m Round Tower is not to be overlooked. The emblem of the city, it was built as a defence tower between 1440 and 1453. The St. Mary Assumption parish church dates back to 11th and 12th centuries and with its four towers it ranks among the most beautiful Roman churches on the Middle Rhine. The "Alter Krahnen" (Old Crane) from 1561 which was in operation up until 1911, is an outstanding sight in Andernach. Another historical building is the town hall from the 16th century.

The "Alter Krahnen" in Andernach

360° Panorama: Andernach – The city castle "Stadtburg" 15

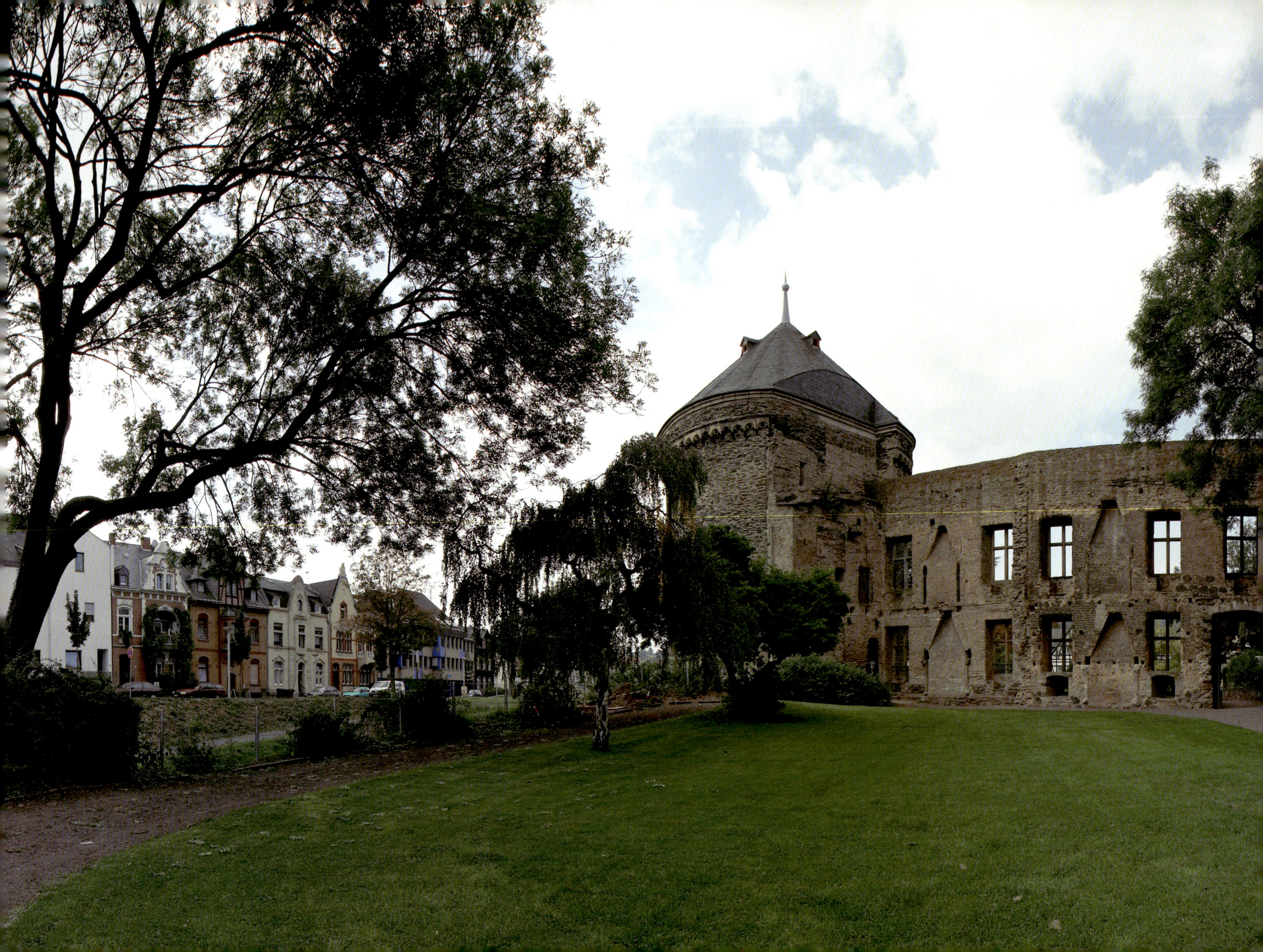

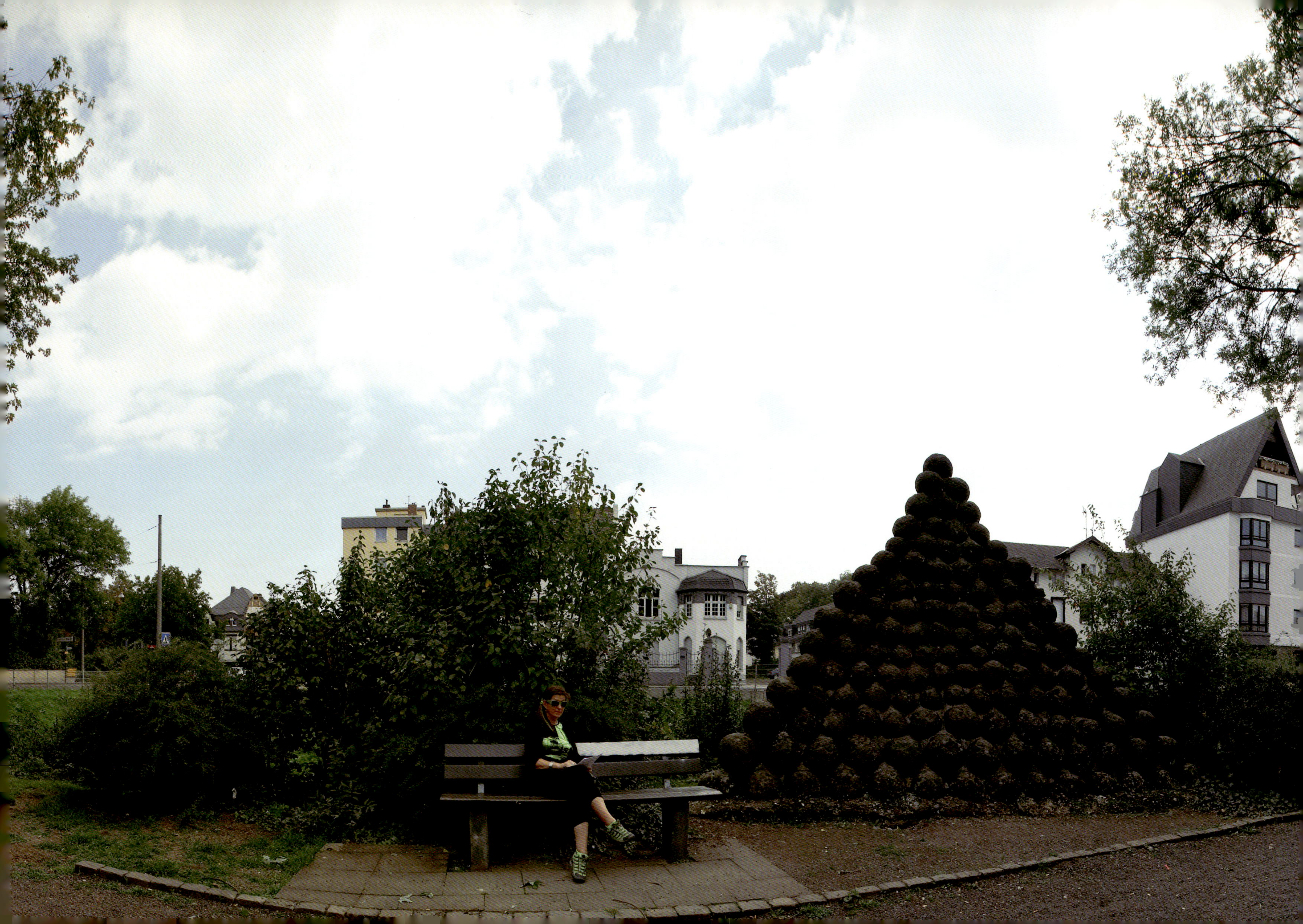

Leutesdorf is a wine and cultural town on the eastern bank of the Rhine. Taxes were first levied there in 1309 and the "Zolltor" (Toll Gate) was built in 1690. The town's entire Rhine shore draws visitors with its attractive buildings and half-timbered houses, which served as the stylish backdrop for a television series. The St. Laurentius parish church building from 1730 towers over the town.

In Namedy, on the western bank of the Rhine, stands the castle of the same name. Built as a moated castle in the 14th century, it was expanded into a palatial complex at the end of the 19th century in Historism style. The world's highest cold-water geyser, around 50 m high, bubbles up from the Rhine island Namedyer Werth, which is also a significant bird protection area.

Hammerstein, on the eastern bank of the Rhine, is home to unique witnesses of historical time periods. The Hammerstein ruins from the 10th century are the oldest castle complex in the Middle Rhine valley. The origins of the St. Georg parish church also date back to the 10th century.

The Rhine island Hammersteiner Werth, which boasts a beautiful sandy beach, lies outside of the wine town of Hammerstein.

St. Suitbertus parish church is located in Rheinbrohl, north of Hammerstein, and was built from 1852 to 1856. The Gertrude Chapel from the 13th century features an ornate altar from the 17th century. The "Gertrudenhof", the historic town hall, dates back to the 7th century. A small Roman fort is located in the Rheinbrohl area. The 2nd century AD fortification complex was discovered in 1899.

Brohleck Castle is located in Brohl-Lützing on the western bank of the Rhine. It was built in 1891 on the site of another castle from the 14th century.

The nearby castle of Schweppenburg was first mentioned in documents in 1365 and was rebuilt from 1637 to 1639 and belongs to family Geyr von Schweppenburg today.

Rheineck Castle, situated between Brohl-Lützing and Bad Breisig, is one of the most famous historical sights on the Rhine. Built in the 11th century by the Rhenish count palatines, it had been destroyed and rebuilt multiple times until the 18th century. In 1832 the complex was taken over by Bonn university professor August von Bethmann-Hollweg, who had renowned Koblenz master builder Claudius de Lassaulx reconstruct it according to the original floor plans.

City castle "Stadtburg" Andernach

Bad Hönningen, which is located on the eastern bank of the Rhine in the direct vicinity of the Limes, dates back to Roman times and was first mentioned in documents in 1019. Springs containing carbonic acid were discovered there at the end of the 19th century. Bad Hönningen is the therapeutic epicentre of the Kristall-Rheinpark thermae.

The idyllic town boasts incomparable attractions. The "Hohe Haus" (High House) was built in 1438 and now houses a municipal museum. The "Tempelhof" dates back to 1225, the "Burghaus" on the Rhine to the 17th century and was once Hönningen's first post station.

Ariendorf Castle, located in the Ariendorf quarter, is a neo-Gothic building from 1840 that is reinforced with merlons and corner towers. The castle is located above the town and the complex dates back to a mediaeval castle. Arenfels Castle has 365 windows, 52 doors and 12 towers. The Ariendorf "Pegelturm", a water gauge tower, was built in 1900 and is one of the last of its kind in the region.

Nearby Leubsdorf, which is primarily known for its red wine, is home to the Saint Walburgis parish church – also known as the "White Church of the Rhine". It was built on a cliff in 1905.

The "Burghaus" was constructed in the 16th century but dates back to 13th century.

The spa town of Bad Breisig on the western bank of the Rhine which has existed as a settlement since Roman and Franconian times, is known for its thermal springs. It is home to the "Altes Zollhaus" (old toll house), built in 1500, the Old Town Hall with a doll museum from the 19th century, as well as the symbol of the city, the Saint Mary's Church which was built from 1717 to 1725. Relaxation is guaranteed at the idyllic spa park with its exotic tree population. The Bad Breisig fairytale forest is another unique attraction in the town.

Sinzig lies on the western bank of the Rhine at the mouth of Ahr River. From the 12th to the 14th century, it was the seat of an imperial palace and host to numerous kings and emperors, including Frederick I. Barbarossa, to whom the town owes its nickname "Barbarossa City". A margrave's water castle was built in 1348 on the site where the mid 19th century Sinzig Castle now stands. Today, the complex serves as a museum. It was placed under monument protection in 1988 along with the picturesque castle garden. A bridge over the Ahr leads to the small town of Kripp near Remagen.

Arenfels Castle in Bad Hönningen

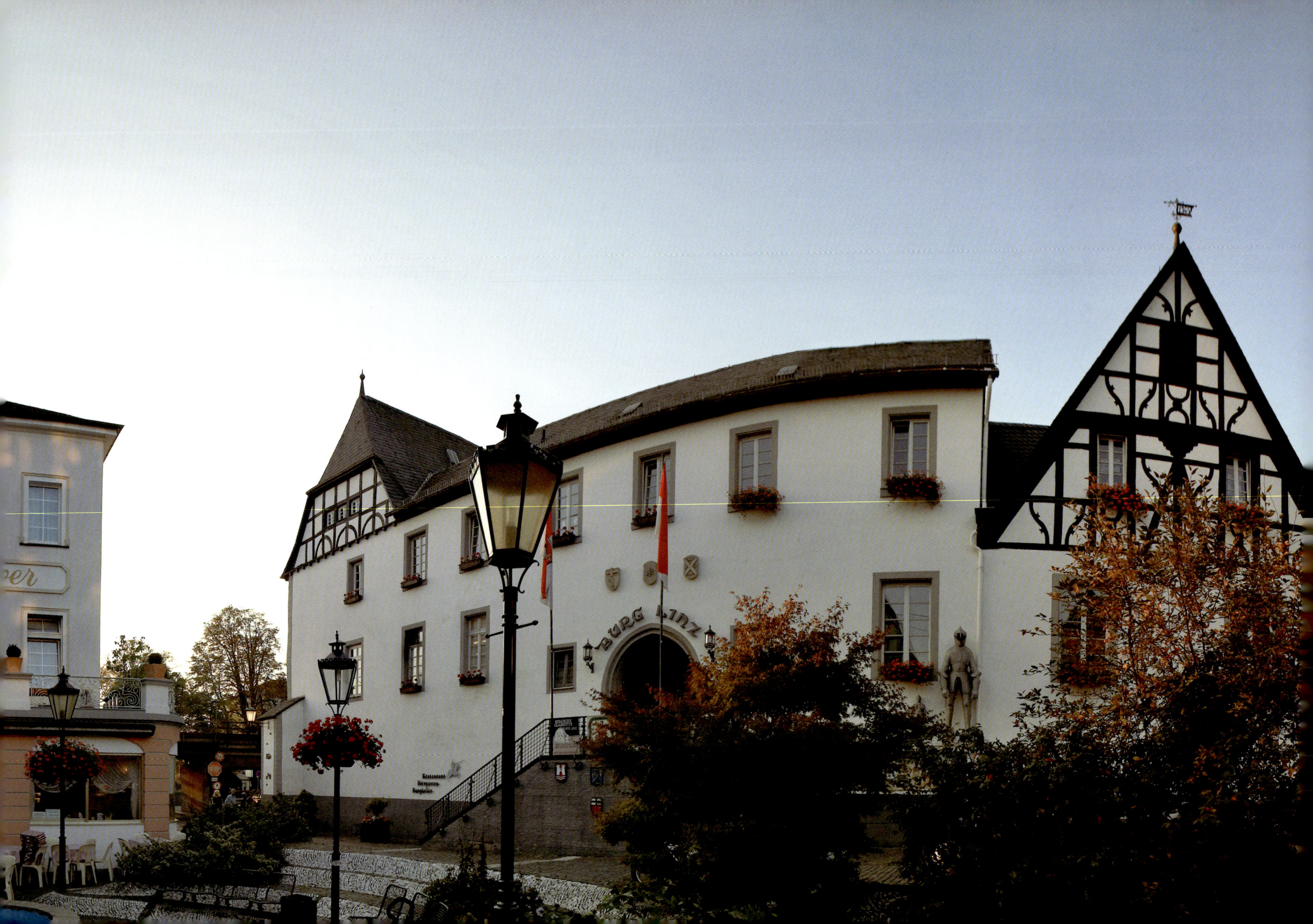
BURG LINZ

LINZ
Castle Square

Linz on the eastern bank of the Rhine is called the "Colourful town on the Rhine" because of the numerous brightly coloured half-timbered houses in the Old Town. First mentioned in public records in 874 as "Lincesce," grave findings from early Franconian times prove that it was an important early settlement. After receiving its city charter in 1320, imposing city fortification walls rose up with gates, some of which remain intact as the large Rheintor. In addition to ornate citizen's houses from five centuries, there are also new buildings in traditional half-timbered style. One of the most prominent squares is the Castle Square with "Strünzerbrunnen" which is meant to be an embodiment – albeit a slightly exaggerated one – of the character of Linz residents. The town hall from the 14th century is also located at the Burgplatz. Linz Castle which was built in 1365, is an interesting sight with its octagonal tower. It features a Roman glassworks in the style of 2,000 years ago, an authentic torture chamber in a dungeon and traditional cuisine in a faithful reproduction in the knights' hall.
Ockenfels Castle – originally called zur Leyen Castle- is situated on a bank in the nearby town of Ockenfels. Built in the early 13th century, it is now privately owned.
The Kasbach flows through Kasbach-Ohlenberg, north of Linz. In 1356 it marked the border between the electorates of Trier and Cologne and today it geographically separates the Diocese of Trier from the Archbishopric of Cologne. Saint Nicholas Church in the Ohlenberg district was built in neo-Roman style in 1903 preserving the 17th century tower of an older structure.

The "Strünzerbrunnen" fountain at the Castle Square

360° Panorama: Linz – Castle Square **16**

Steffens Pilsener
Restaurant
Steffens Pilsener
Café-Gelateria
Rico
Pizza & Eis
CAFE COND

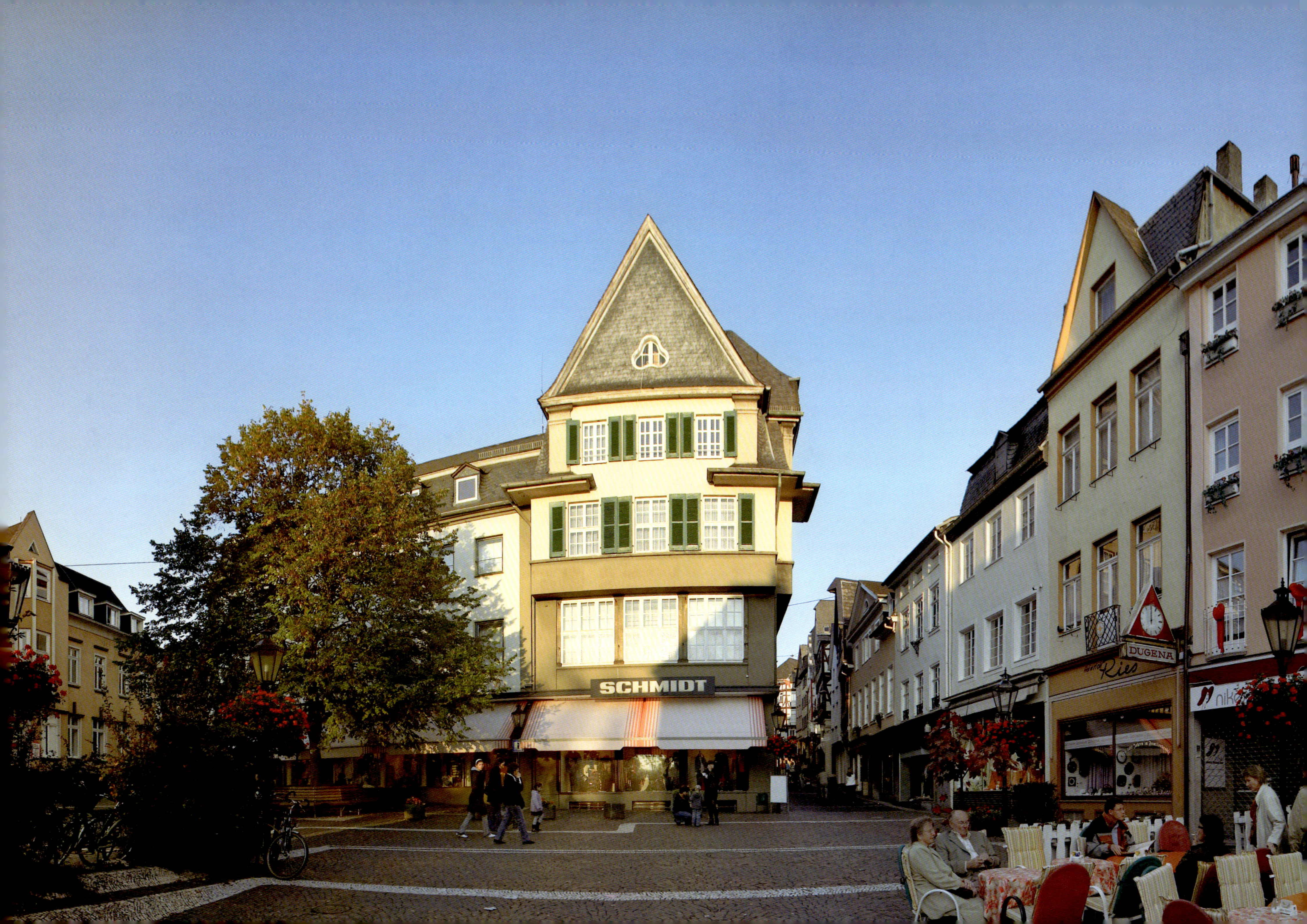
SCHMIDT
Ries
DUGENA

The Linz market place

Linz Castle Square

The wine-growing town of Kripp is situated opposite to Linz. It was first mentioned in documents in 1474 and was an important towing navigation station. The present-day Remagen quarter of Kripp features a romantic Rhine promenade. You cannot miss the town's symbol, the water tower from 1904 which is under monument protection.

Erpel on the eastern bank of the Rhine looks back on 1,500 years of history. The idyllic town centre is home to many diverse historical witnesses that are worth seeing, for example the market place with its half-timbered houses, the town hall from 1780 and the 13th century Saint Severinus Church. The Neutor gate from 1420 is part of the city fortification that has been preserved to this day. The former east portal of the Bridge of Remagen on the banks of the Rhine should not be missed. The mighty Erpeler Ley basalt cliff ranks among the most striking cliffs on the Rhine.

Nearby Unkel was first mentioned in documents in 886. The eye-catching Rhine promenade which is lined with linden trees, features the imposing Freiligrath house from 1760, where the poet lived from 1839 to 1841. The old Saint Pantaleon parish church from the 13th century is a town jewel.

The Scheuren chapel, built around 1500, is located at Scheuren's village square. The Unkel prison tower "Gefängnisturm" is another emblem of the town. Vilzelt Castle which was first mentioned in public records in the 13th century, is a former water castle in the Heister quarter.

The Unkelstein moutain range is located across from Unkel on the western bank of the Rhine. It made the news in 1846 when a massive landslide caused by a stone pit below the mountain "Birgeier Kopf" occurred which was burying wide parts of the surrounding area.

Visitors to Oberwinter enjoy the beautiful old buildings and the "ahl Pump", a water pump from 1780.

Top: View from the Erpeler Ley; Bottom: The Bridge of Remagen and Erpel's town centre

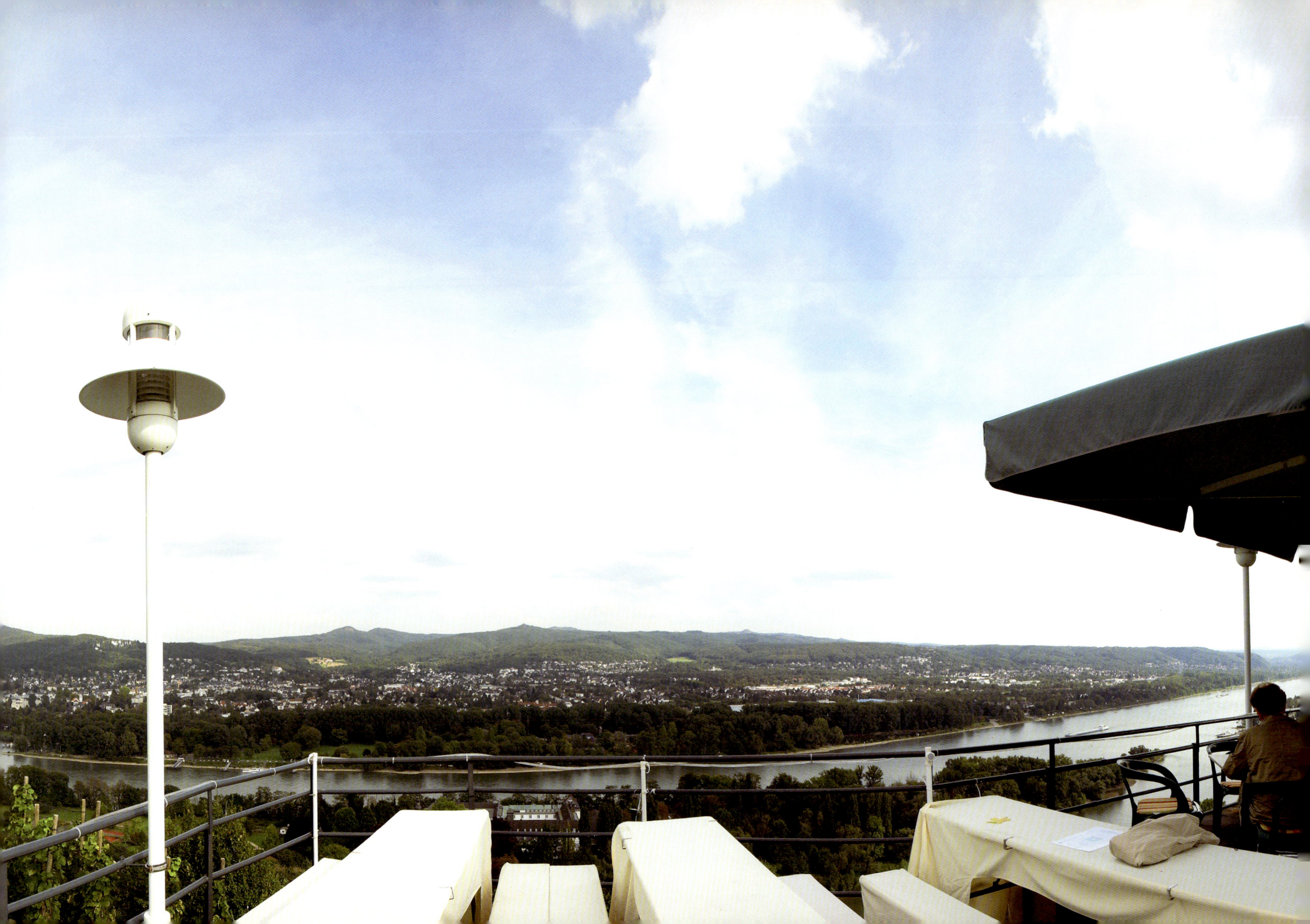

REMAGEN

Rolandsbogen

Remagen is located on the western bank of the Rhine and was built on top of the approximately 2.000-year-old Roman castle "Rigomagus" which was excavated in 1902. Remagen had a town charter as early as 1221 and was fortified at the end of the 14th century. A connection was made on the Cologne–Koblenz railway line in the mid 19th century under Prussian rule. The Ludendorff railway bridge was built over the Rhine in World War I which had a critical impact on the outcome of World War II and is known as the "Bridge of Remagen". The bridge towers now house the Peace Museum. The St. Peter and Paul parish church from 1003 is also worth seeing.

The Rolandsbogen is located high above the Rhine valley on a precipice of the Rodderberg. Overgrown with ivy, it is the only relic of the former Rolandseck Castle. This "Höhenburg" castle which was built in 1122, fell down to the foundation walls in 1673 because of an earthquake. Only one arched window survived: The later by invocation of poet Freiligrath restored "Rolandsbogen" (Roland's Arch").

In the Hentzenpark on the Rolandswerth Rhine shore, artists created the Secret Gardens Rolandswerth, part of the open-air sculpture exposition "Skulpturenufer Remagen".

The Rolandseck railway station in Rolandswerth from 1856 has housed a museum since 2007.

A convent that dates back to 1148 is located upstream on the island of Nonnenwerth.

Steeped in history, the Church of Saint Apollinaris stands on a bank known today as Apollinarisberg, north of Remagen. Around the end of the 14th century, the relics of Saint Apollinaris supposedly arrived at the Benedictine provost residence, then situated on the mountain, whereby the church became a pilgrimage site. After the dissolution of the provost, a new church building was planned and built in 1842 according to the plans of the architect of the Cologne Cathedral Ernst Friedrich Zwirner.

Marienfels Castle is located between Remagen and Oberwinter to the north. It is a romantic 19th century building surrounded by a vast park.

Church of Saint Apollinaris above Remagen

360°-Panoramafoto: Remagen – Rolandsbogen **17**

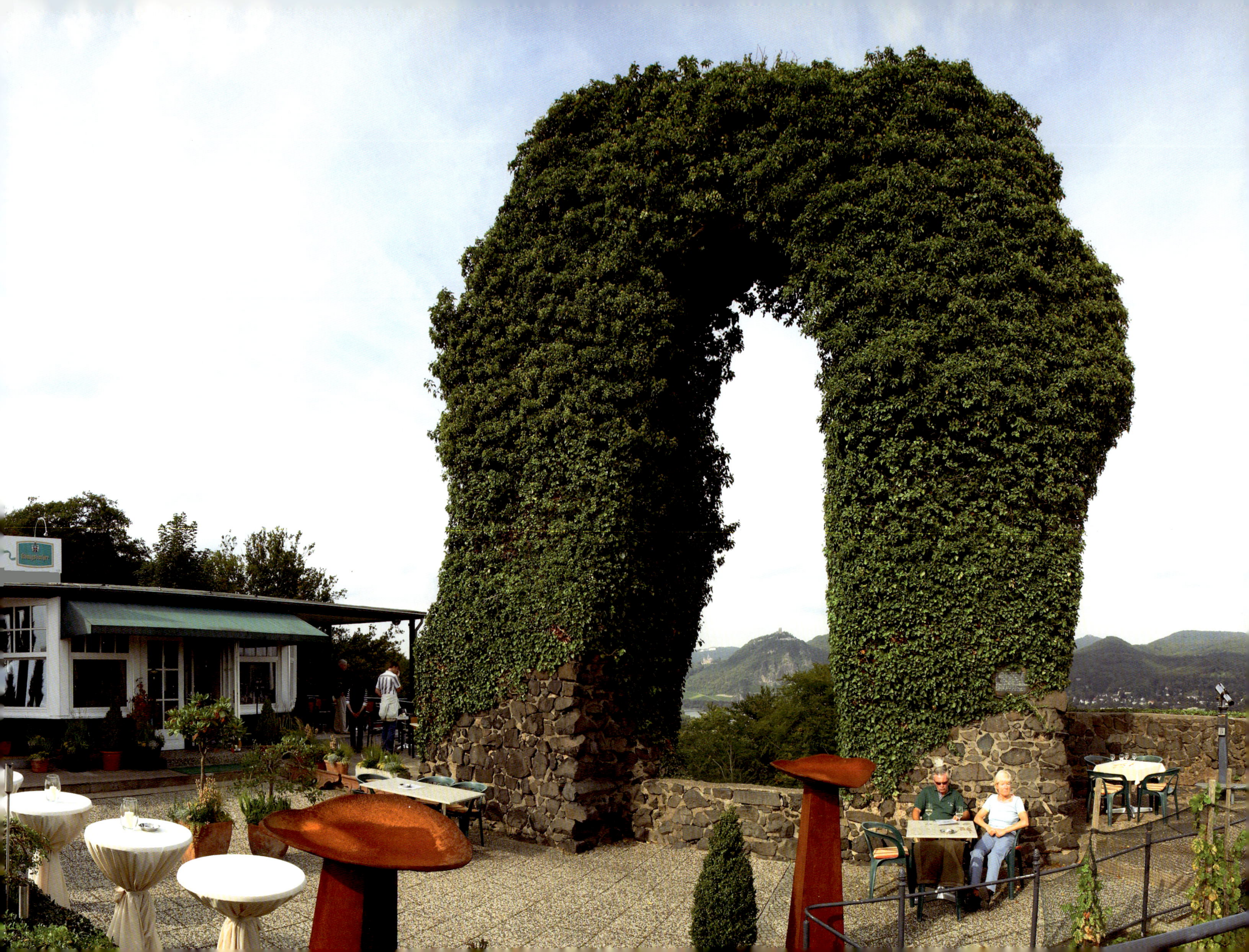

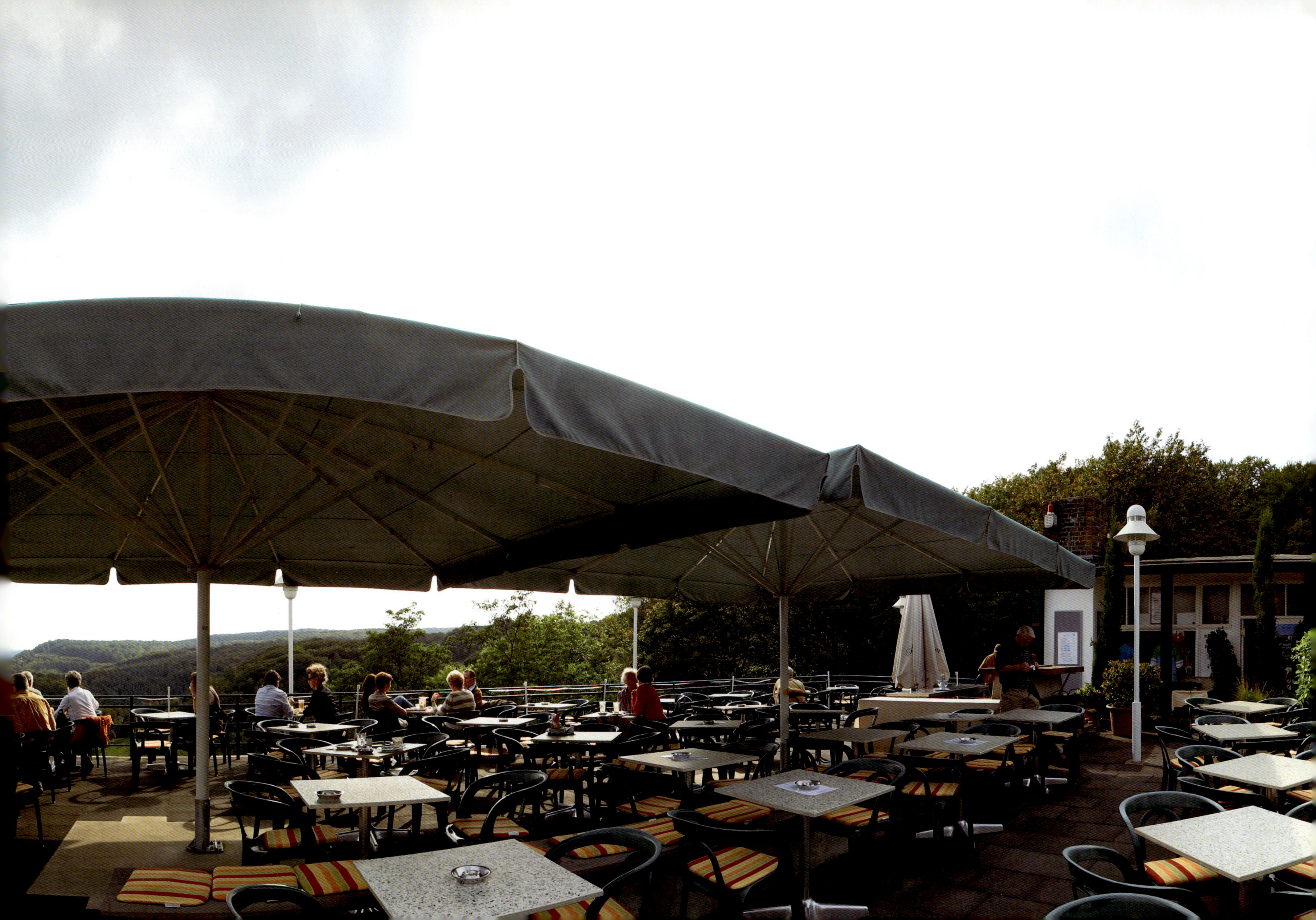

Rheinbreitbach on the eastern bank of the Rhine looks back on more than 1,000 years of history, as reflected in the town centre with its historical half-timbered houses, wineries and ornate villas. A model of the late Gothic parish church Saint Mary Magdalene from the 15th and 16th centuries is displayed in the Louvre as an example of a Rhenish village church.

The 17th century Leonardus Chapel which was a well known pilgrimage church in earlier times, is also worth seeing. The ruins of the "Untere Burg" (the lower castle) have been preserved to this day. Located near the parish church, it is one of the oldest water castles in Germany. The "Obere Burg" (the upper castle) was carefully restored and stands amidst a splendid park. The building became famous at the beginning of the 20th century when writer Rudolf Herzog resided there.

The Siebengebirge (seven mountains) mountain range with its majestic forests emerged around 25.5 million years ago in the Oligocene period. It ranks among the oldest nature protection areas in Germany and stretches east of the Rhine all the way to Bonn. At 460 m, the Große Ölberg reaches the highest elevation in the Siebengebirge, which consists of 40 mountains and is of volcanic origin. The other six out of the seven highest mountains are: Löwenburg, on which stands a 12th century castle ruin of the same name, Lohrberg at 435 m, Nonnenstromberg at 335 m, Petersberg at 331 m, Wolkenburg at 324 m with a ruin of the same name, and Drachenfels at 320 m, on which a restaurant is located next to a castle ruin.

The first Roman quarries emerged on Siebengebirge in the 1st century AD, but mining there came to a standstill starting in 1875.

View of Bad Godesberg and Godesburg Castle

Bad Honnef, north of Linz, was first mentioned in documents in 922 as "Hunapha." The first mineral spring was discovered there in 1897, and from then the town was allowed to use "Bad" (spa) in its name.

Numerous sights have survived to this day, including the parish church Saint John Baptist originating in the 12th century, the old sexton house right next door and the parish hall. Visitors marvel at the Saint Martin Church, built in 1968 in the Selhof quarter, and at the 18th century "Maria Heimsuchung" Chapel in Rhöndorf. Other outstanding buildings include the 13th century "Haus im Turm" (the house in a tower), the former spa building that is now a convention facility with the Villa Haarhaus and the Konrad Adenauer house with its renowned rose garden. The island of Grafenwerth is the most famous public park in Bad Honnef.

The small adjacent town of Mehlem has Franconian roots and is just outside the city limits of Bonn. It is known for its idyllic Rhine promenade. Mehlem's town centre is dominated by the 12th century Saint Severin parish church.

The striking Godesburg Castle stands on a hilltop in Bad Godesberg. The castle was built in the 13th century and was used as an electoral stronghold and residence in the Middle Ages. It was demolished in 1583, and the ruins were restored in 1960. It now houses a hotel and restaurant.

Top: Rhöndorf Chapel in Bad Honnef; bottom: Ferries between Königswinter and Bad Godesberg

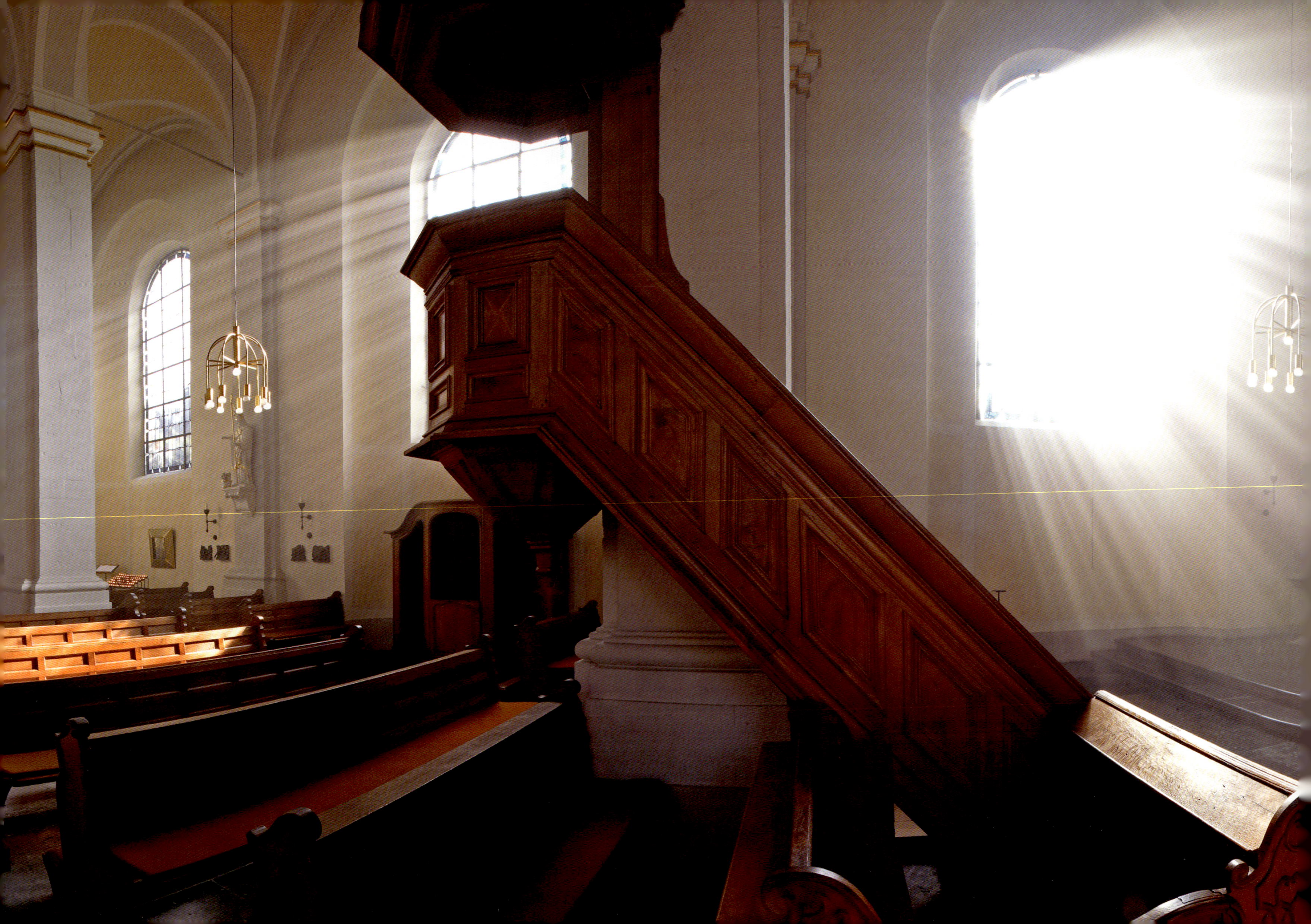

KÖNIGSWINTER

Drachenfels

Königswinter, opposite to Bonn district Bad Godesberg and on the eastern bank of the Rhine, is a lively city with many faces. It enjoys an idyllic setting framed by the Rhine and the legendary Siebengebirge. The town woos visitors not only with its surrounding scenic beauty, but also its numerous historical monuments and buildings.

Nearby Drachenfels, on which the Romans operated quarries, became the first property in Germany to be placed under nature protection in 1836. Although it is not the highest mountain in the Siebengebirge at 321 m, Drachenfels is the most famous. This is the site of the battle between Siegfried and the dragon. The oldest rack railway in Germany has been going up to Drachenfels since 1883, where staggering panorama views are guaranteed. The ruins of 12th century castle Drachenfels stand atop of the mountain of the same name. The castle was occupied by the burgraves of Drachenfels until the 16th century, after which it fell into increasing disrepair. It became the property of the Prussian regime in 1836, and since then various activities have been taken to preserve the ruins. It represents one of the pre-eminent symbols of Rhine romanticism and draws visitors from all over the world. Drachenburg Castle nearby Drachenfels is another Königswinter monumental historic building and tourist landmark. Built from 1882 to 1884, the castle has experienced a very changeful history. Facing impending deterioration, the complex was lavishly restored in recent years and now houses a museum on the history of nature protection in Germany

Drachenfels with castle ruins of Drachenfels and Drachenburg Castle

360° Panorama: Königswinter – Church St. Remigius **18**

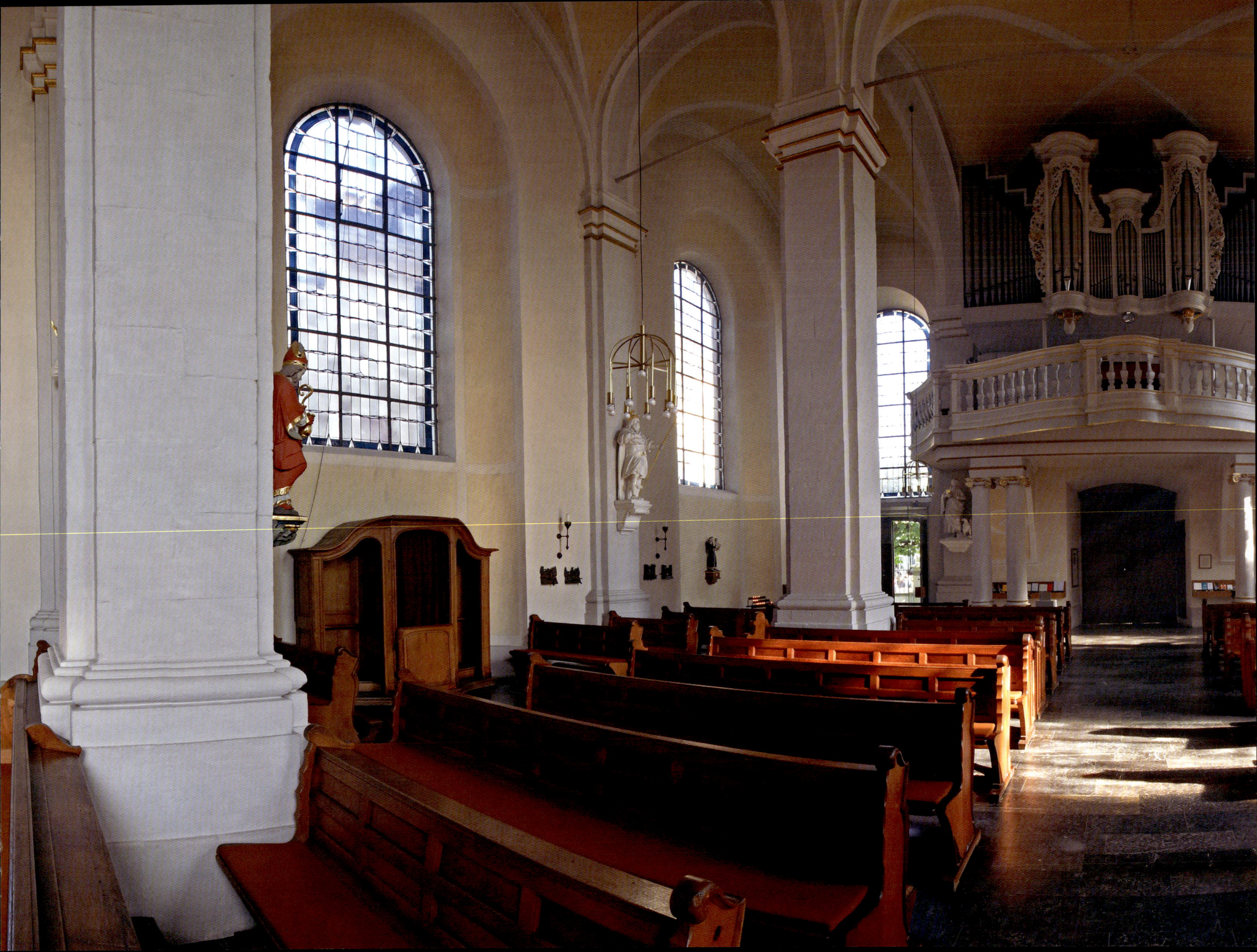

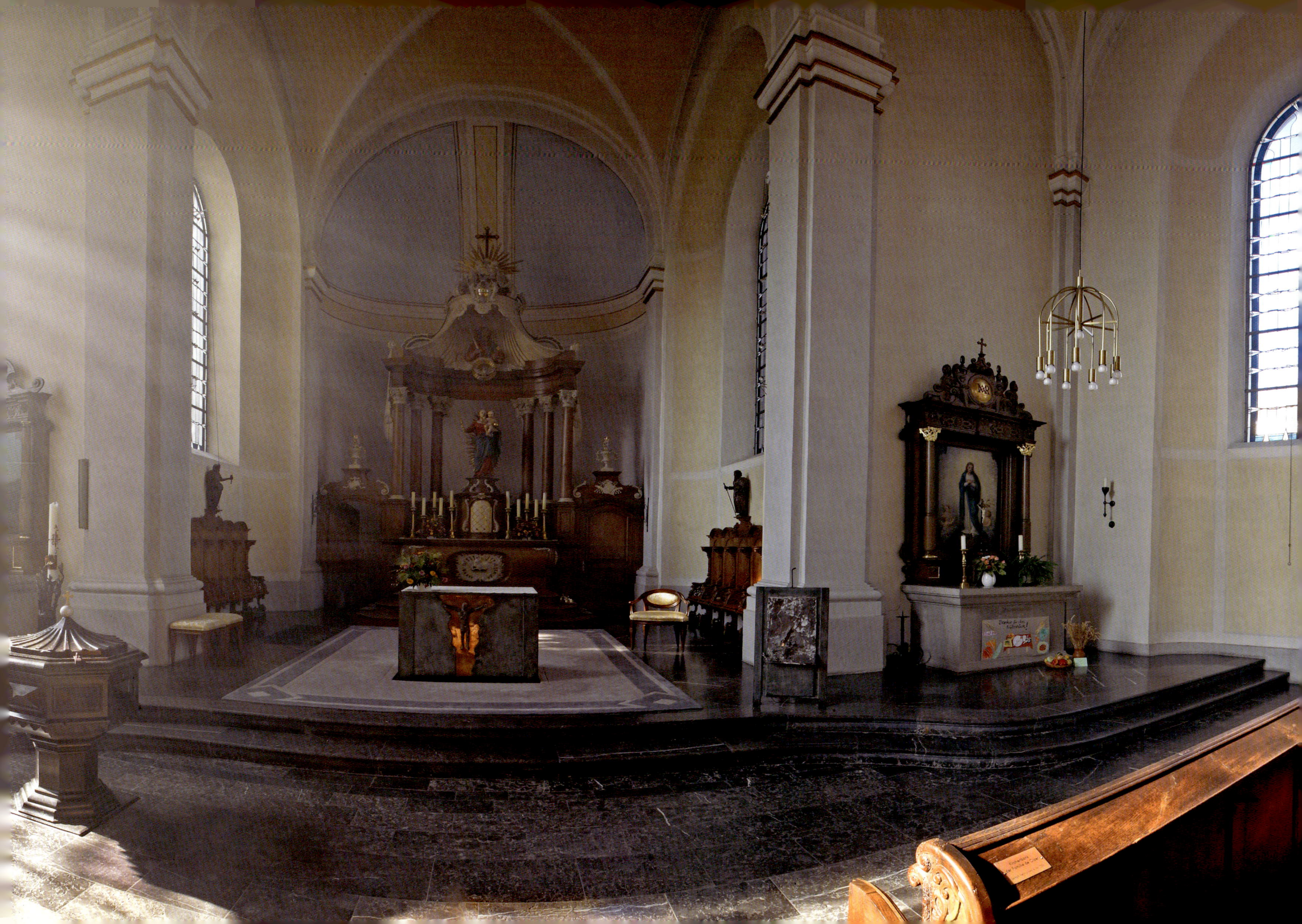

In Petersberg, northeast of Königswinter, the noble hotel that opened in 1892 served as the residence for state guests up until the 1970's. The lovingly restored hotel has been the official guesthouse of the Federal Republic of Germany since 1990.

"Ofenkaulen," a late mediaeval tunnel system, is an archaeological monument located in Siebengebirge, north of Königswinter. Trachyte tuff is mined there for making Königswinter ovens, which are well known all over Europe. Today, the Ofenkaulen is one of the most important bat reservations in the region.

The first indications of a settlement in Königswinter date back to the 7th century. Winetre, the present-day Königswinter, was first mentioned in documents in 1015. The name "Winetre" suggests that wine was cultivated in the region back then. Although Königswinter as it was officially named in 1342, did not have a town charter, it did have its own fortification. Numerous cultural landmarks document the town's historical development, including its fascinating church and monastery buildings.

The Roman provost church Propsteikirche in Oberpleis quarter is one of them. It features a crypt and impressive cloister from the 12th century.

A baroque house built in 1732 houses the Siebengebirge museum in Königswinter. With its extensive collections of cultural and historical items, it offers exciting insights into life in that region. The "Haus Schlesien", located in a roughly 800-year-old former soccage farm, is a centre for Silesian culture.

Cistercian monks founded an abbey in the Heisterbach quarter around 1200. A short time later, an imposing church which has been the second largest Romanesque structure in Rhineland behind Cologne Cathedral, emerged there of which only the choir ruins remain.

Königswinter decorated for a wine festival

Oberdollendorf, a northly part of Königswinter, is home to the Brückenhofmuseum. Located in a 17th century winery, the museum beckons visitors to stop by. Countless guests also come to see Sea Life Königswinter, a spectacular sea water aquarium.

Rüngsdorf, which is a part of Bonn, is located across from Königswinter. It boasts a beautiful Rhine promenade, and the historic Rheinhotel Dreesen catches the eye with its ornate Art Nouveau facade.

Rüngsdorf is characterised by numerous villas built by prosperous figures in the 19th century. The town's main attraction is the old Rüngsdorf church tower, which was built around 1200 and forms part of the Saint Andrew's Church from the early 20th century. The Saint Mary's Chapel which probably dates back to the end of the 18th century has been placed under monument protection.

Deichmannsaue Castle is located on the southern end of Rüngsdorf. The main building which was rebuilt in 1910 on the "Auerhof" from 1662, and after World War II confiscated by the allied forces, has housed various German Federal Government facilities for more than five decades.

Königswinter wine festival

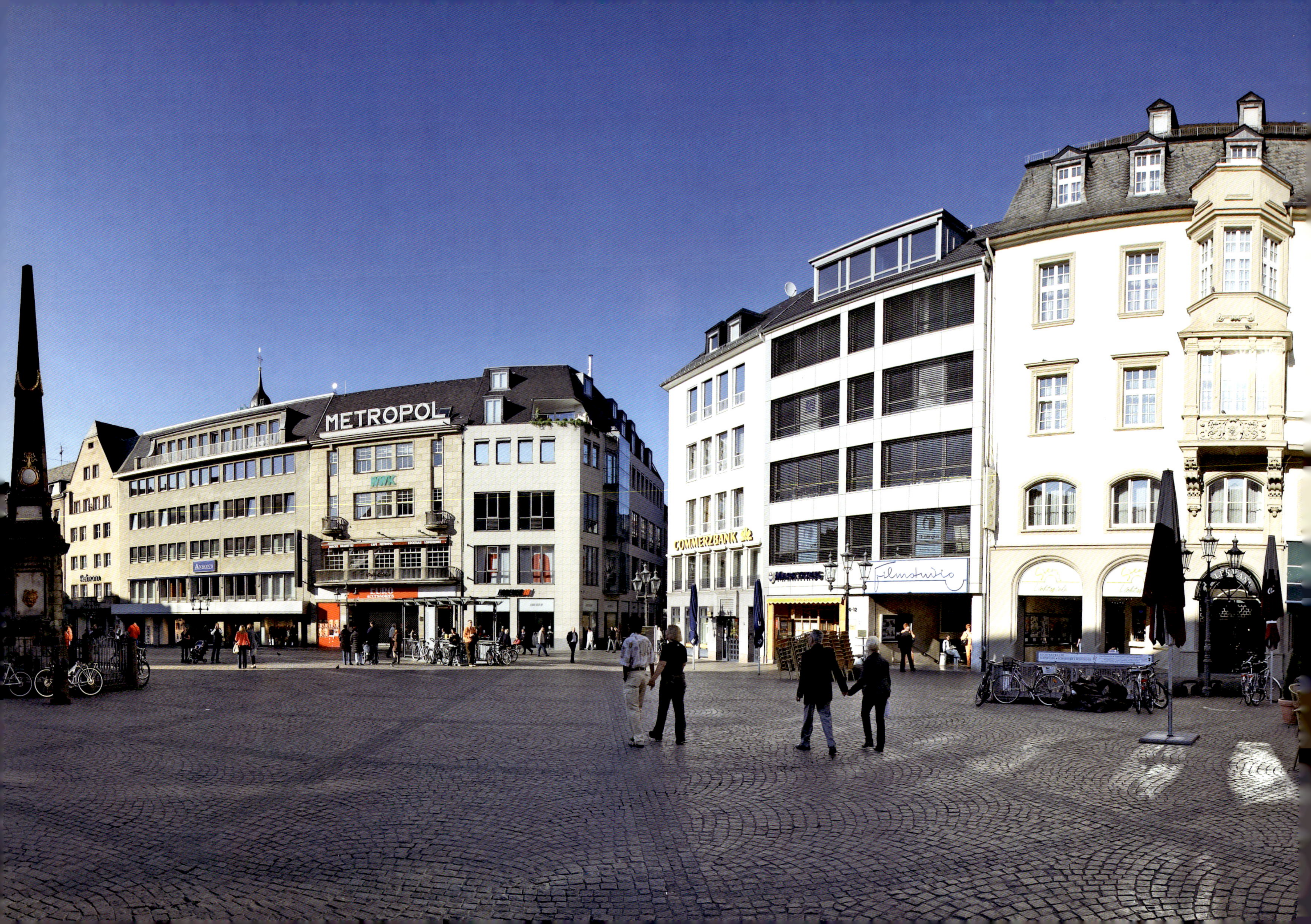
METROPOL
COMMERZBANK
Filmstudio

BONN

Market Place

The Market Place with its fountain from 1777, is the pulsating heart of Bonn to present day. It forms an atmospheric backdrop to open-air events such as the famous "Bonn Summer" festival. Bonn's 2,000-year history can be traced back to Roman times.

Craftsmen and merchants settled next to a fortified encampment. The name of the settlement, "vicus Bonnensis" refers to the city's later name. Numerous valuable findings bear witness to the Roman presence in the present-day urban area.

From the end of the 16th century to 1794, Bonn was the capital city and residence of the Elector of Cologne, and was the capital city of the Federal Republic of Germany from 1949 until 1990.

Visitors find interesting traces of Bonn's great past all over the city. The old Town Hall which was built starting in 1737 in Rococo style, is one of its symbols. Right next door is the grandiose Prince-electorate castle Kurfürstliches Schloss from the 16th and 17th centuries.

Bonn Town Hall

360° Panorama: Bonn – Market Place **19**

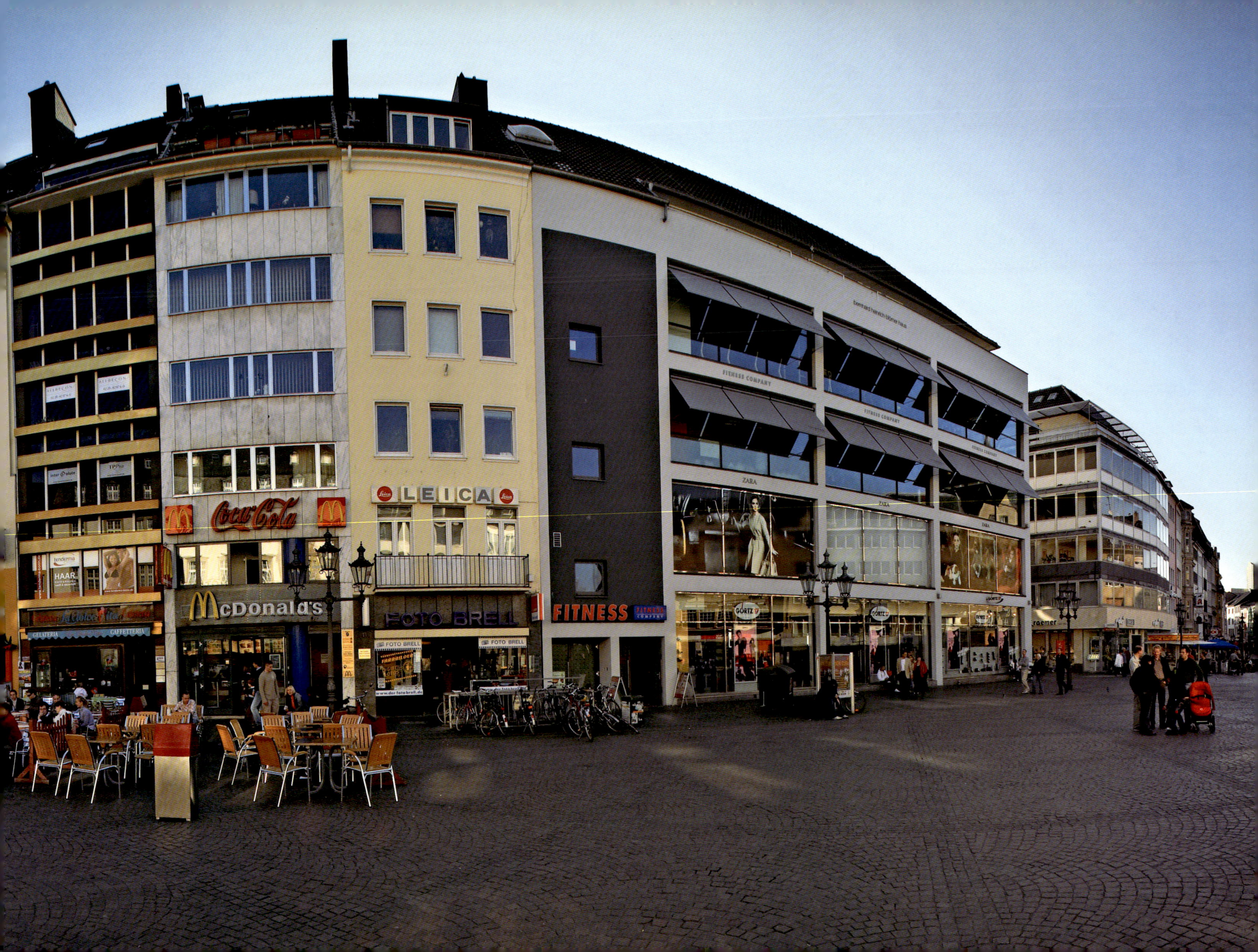
Coca-Cola
McDonald's
LEICA
FOTO BRELL
FITNESS

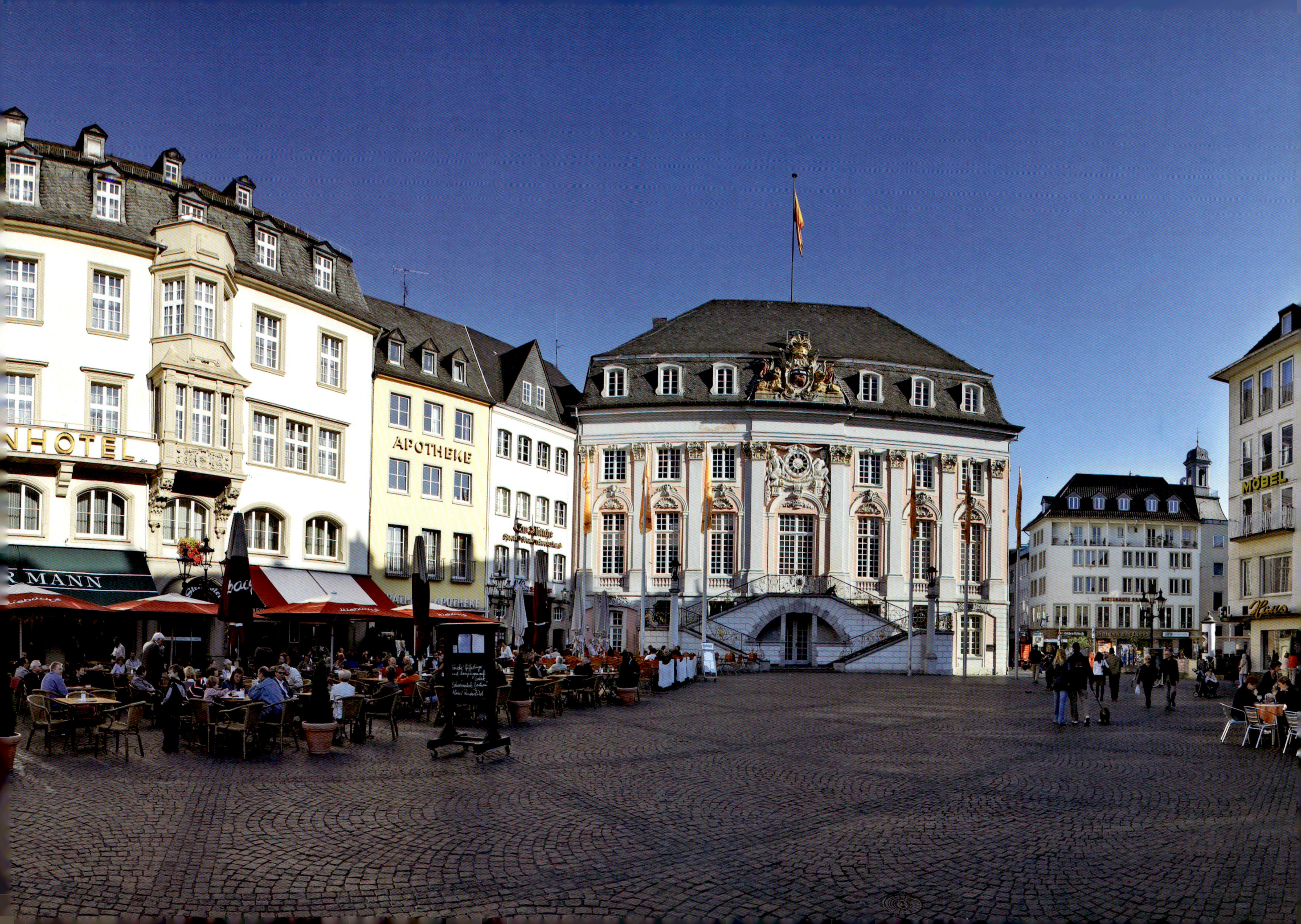
NHOTEL
R MANN
APOTHEKE
MÖBEL

The station building of Bonn's central station, which was built from 1883-1884, is under monument protection. A stroll along Poppelsdorfer Allee will take you to the station, from where you can reach magnificent Poppelsdorfer Palace from the 18th century.

Among the many church buildings in the city, the Bonn Minster is of particular importance. The Romanesque building, a "Papal Basilica minor", dates back to the 11th century and boasts an inexhaustible plethora of sacred art treasures and sight – including the rare Baroque peal of eight historic bells.

The old custom station "Alter Zoll" from the 17th century is a bastion of a former city fortification located on the banks of the Rhine. Bonn is also home to a multitude of prominent museums, including the Art and Exhibition Hall of the Federal Republic of Germany and the Museum of the History of the Federal Republic of Germany, both of which rank among the most visited museums in Germany.

Today, the 394 m long Kennedy Bridge stands in the site of the former 19th century Rhine Bridge. The notorious "Brückenmännchen" sculpture is located on the Bonn side, sending a neighbourly greeting to Beuel on the opposite shore. The Beuel quarter is the historic birthplace of the Rhenish carnival as the Weiberfastnacht (Women's carnival) was born there in 1824. The Vilich quarter in Bonn is located northeast of Beuel and is home to Lede, a water castle whose origins trace back to 1200. The former Roman tower house was expanded into a Gothic castle complex in the 14th century. It was destroyed in the 16th century and was not rebuilt until the beginning of the 20th century.

Ernst Friedrich Wilhelm von Schiller, son of poet and dramatist Friedrich von Schiller, and Maria Magdalena von Pfingsten were married in the Schevasterhof in Vilich, which was built in 1603.

Clemensruhe Palace in Poppelsdorf

Roof of the German Federal Kunsthalle in Bonn

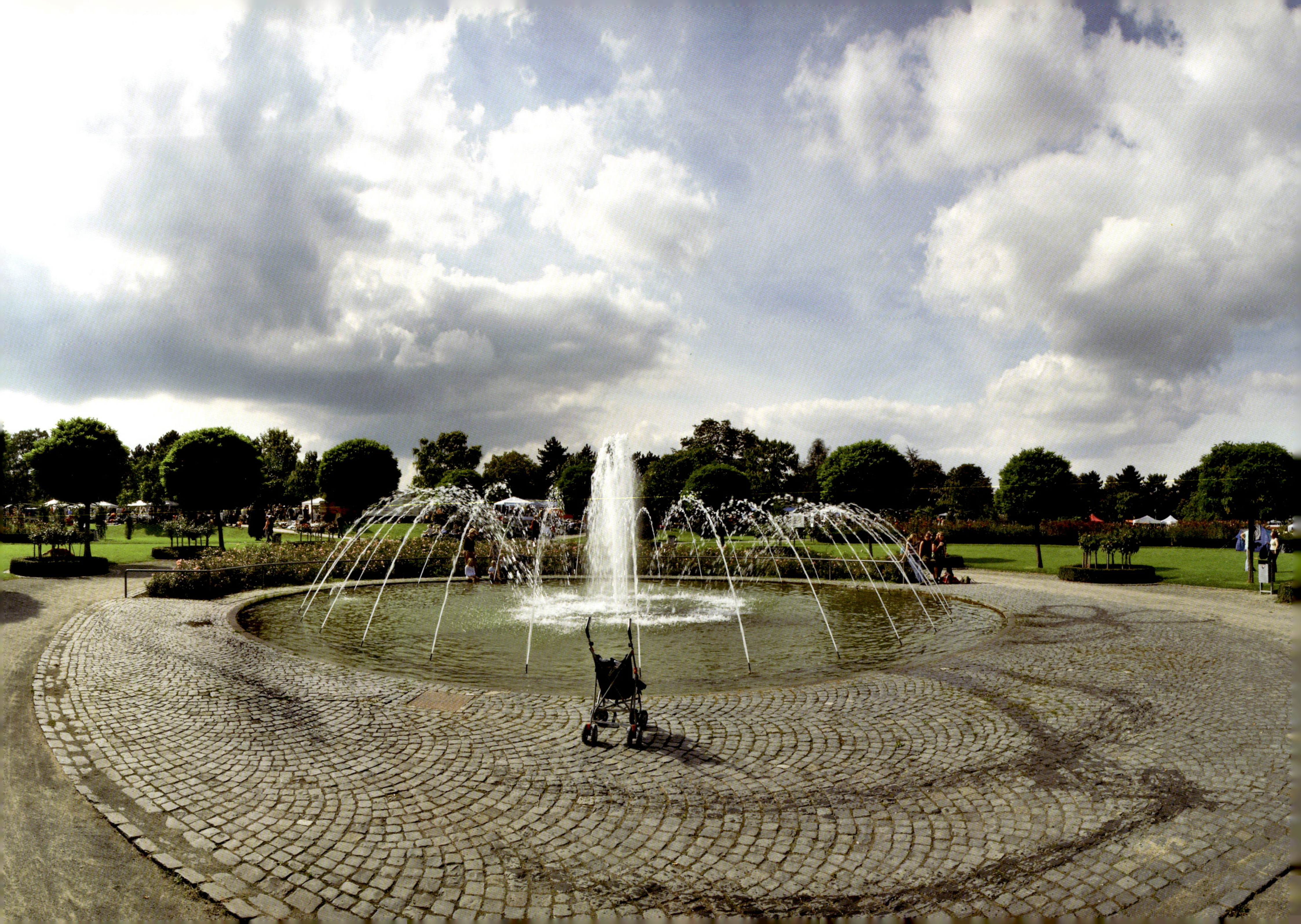

Rheinaue

The leisure park Rheinaue is located in the centre of Bonn's urban area on both sides of the Rhine. Since its founding for the national garden show "Bundesgartenschau" in 1979, it has become a popular local recreation area. With a surface area of 160 ha, the spacious park is almost as big as downtown Bonn. There was originally a riparian forest between Bonn's Gronau quarter and Bad Godesberg's Plittersdorf quarter. Intensive work was done on a large part of this area to make the river navigable.

Every third Saturday of the month between April and October, the Bonn Rheinaue is transformed into a mecca for rummagers and bargain hunters. The 770 m long Konrad-Adenauer Rhine Bridge spans the Rheinaue. Two prominent Bonn buildings can be seen across Rheinaue Lake – the Post Tower, the tallest building in the city at 162.5 m, and the monument-protected "Langer Eugen" (long Eugene), a former office tower for members of parliament since 2006 the centre of the United Nations Campus in the legendary government district. Bonn was once surrounded by no less than 37 castles, of which only a few have been preserved.

Flea market at the Rheinaue

The Post Tower

360° Panorama: Bonn – Rheinaue 20

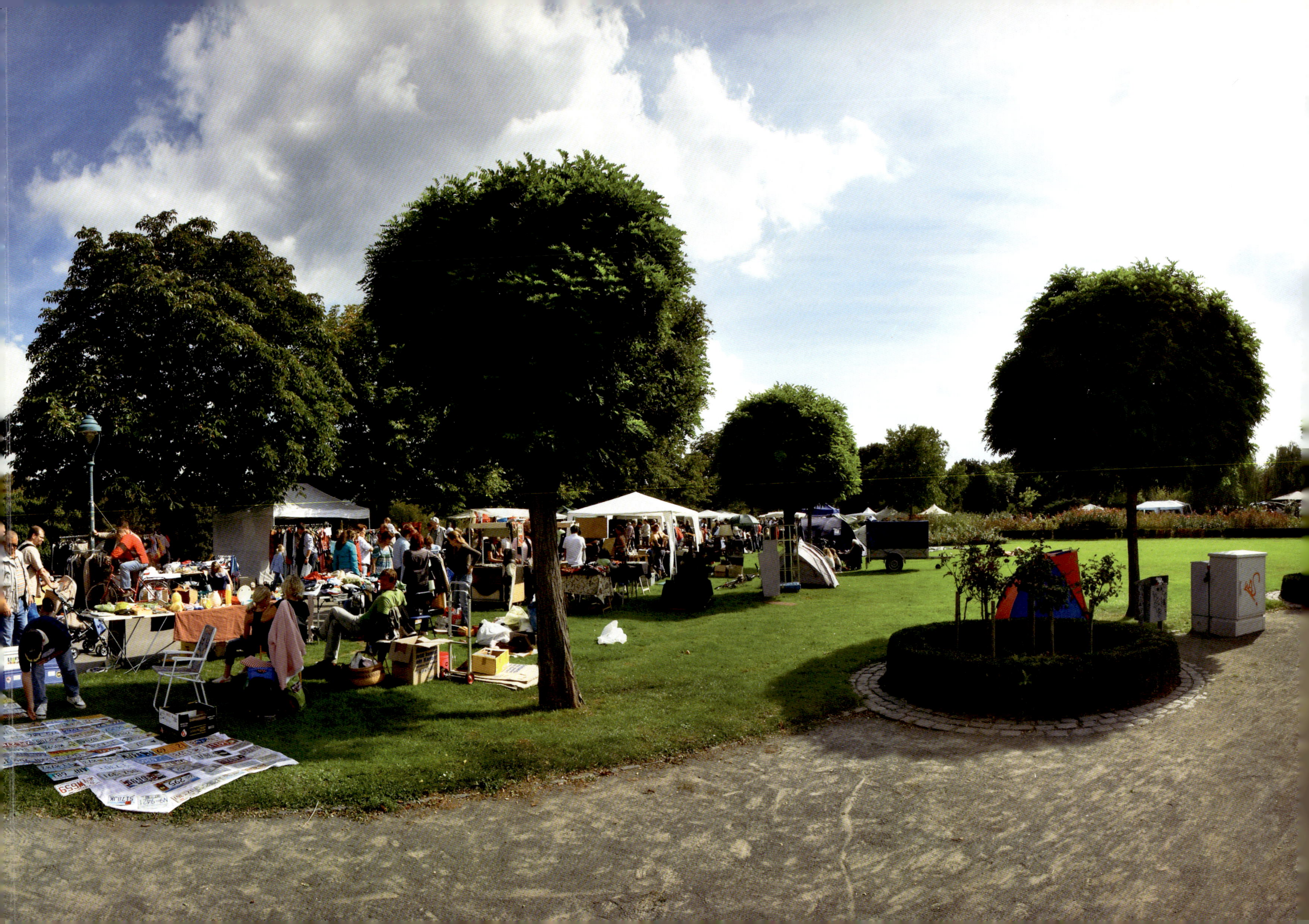

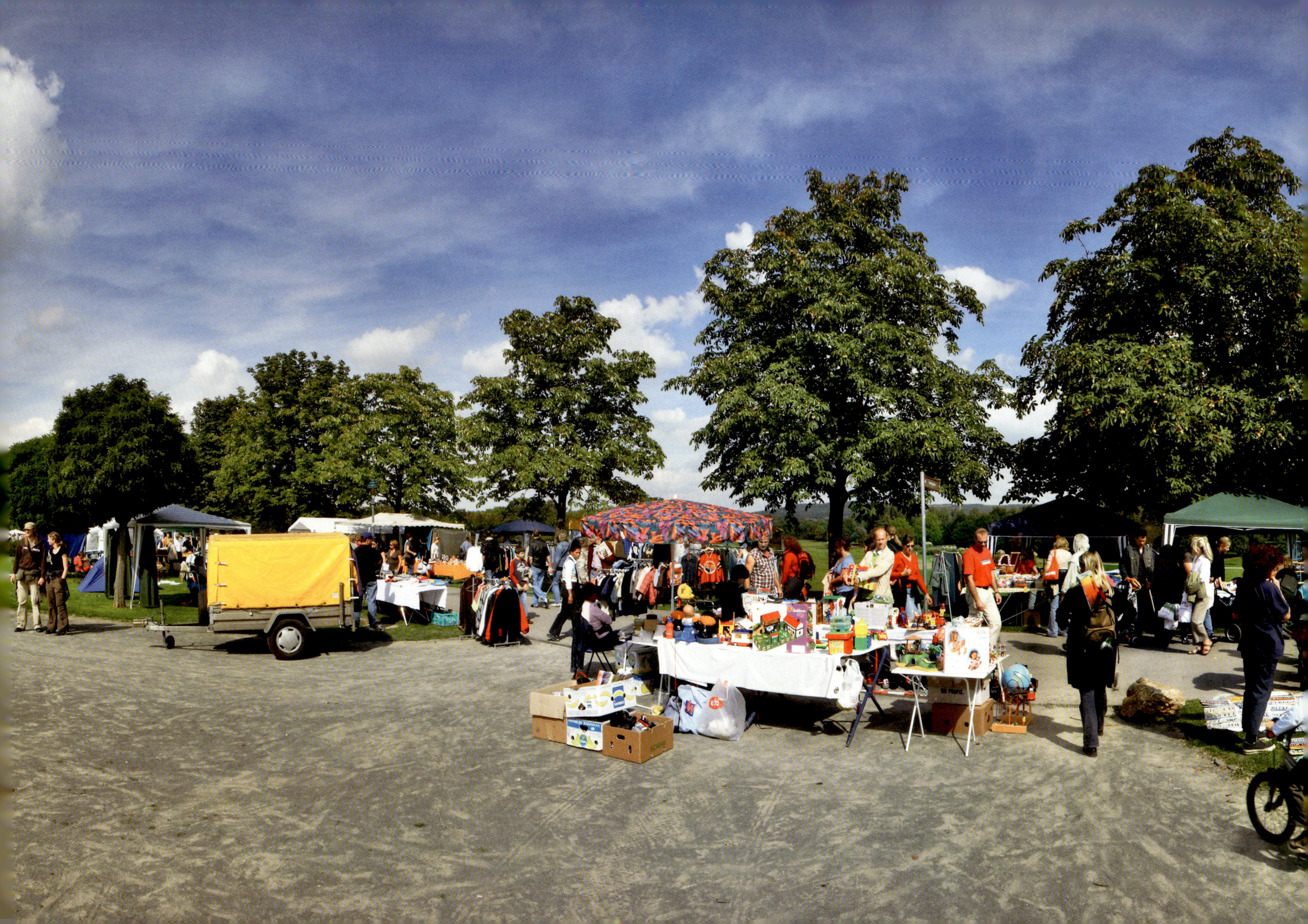

Rheinisches Landesmuseum Bonn

123

Landscape Panoramas 360° – Middle Rhine, 1st Edition

© October 2008, NZVP Books and Calendars Ltd.

ISBN 978-1-877339-72-1

Layout and typesetting	Helga Neubauer, Thorsten Tiedeke (Map)
Text	Norbert Marewski
Photographs	Barbara and Hartmut Röder
Editorial Office	Wolfgang Vorbeck
Translation	StudioTextArt, Frankfurt am Main, Germany
Printed by	Everbest Printing Co Ltd., China

All rights reserved, especially for duplications or dissemination in printed form, or electronic storage in databases, or making available for the public to download, reproduce on a screen or print out by the user. This also relates to pre-releases and excerpts.
We cannot guarantee that this book has not been struck by erronitis. Should this be the case, we would be grateful if you could point out any errors to us. You can contact us at:

NZVP Books and Calendars Ltd.
Level 27, PWC Tower, 188 Quay Street
Auckland, New Zealand
or email us at:
books@nzvp.net

NZVP BOOKS

FRANKFURT AM MAIN, GERMANY · AUCKLAND, NEW ZEALAND